Writing Skills for Readers

日本文化の再発見から学ぶ エッセイの書き方・読み方

Vocabulary to Essay on Japan

日本英語表現学会テキスト研究部会

NAN'UN-DO

音声ファイル
無料 DL
のご案内

このテキストの音声を無料で視聴（ストリーミング）・ダウンロードできます。自習用音声としてご活用ください。
以下のサイトにアクセスしてテキスト番号で検索してください。

https://nanun-do.com　テキスト番号［ **512110** ］

※ 無線 LAN（WiFi）に接続してのご利用を推奨いたします。

※ 音声ダウンロードは Zip ファイルでの提供になります。
お使いの機器によっては別途ソフトウェア（アプリケーション）の導入が必要となります。

Read by

Rachel Walzer（米）
Ryan Drees（米）

※ Writing Skills for Readers 音声ダウンロードページは
以下の QR コードからもご利用になれます。

（執筆者）

新井　巧磨
梅宮　悠
大橋　文香
佐竹　幸信
田村　亮
William Weatherly

Writing Skills for Readers: Vocabulary to Essay on Japan

はじめに

本書は、日本人大学生の英語ライティング力を高めるための教材です。ただし、様々な英語表現を探求する日本英語表現学会のテキスト研究部会が手掛ける教材として、以下のような点で、従来のライティング教材とは異なったアプローチを採りました。

① 本書では可能な限り、「語彙」や「表現」の習得から入る、いわゆるボトムアップ型の学習を意識しました。同時に、昨今のライティング教材の主流である「構造」についても触れています。

② ライティングの手法を学ぶだけでなく、それらが実際の文章中でどのように使われているかを確認できるよう、各 Unit の末尾には比較的難易度の高い reading passage を配置しました。したがって、本書はライティング教材のみならず、状況に応じてリーディング教材としても使用可能です。

③ 著者の手の内（文章を執筆する過程）を見せるような形でライティング指導ができるよう工夫しました。一般的なテキストは画一的な構造やスタイルを学習するものが多いですが、実際のところ、書き手はその都度様々な事柄（その最たるものが「読み手」の存在）に配慮しながらライティングを行っています。本書の著者達も、このことを踏まえて、書き手や読み手の立場を意識しながらテキスト作成を行いました。

これらの特徴を持つ本書が、少しでも効果的な英語ライティング学習／指導の役に立てば、著者一同これに勝る喜びはありません。なお、内容に関しましては、本書のタイトルが示すように、日本文化の再発見をテーマとしました。2020 年の東京オリンピックは、世界的なコロナウィルス感染の影響で延期となりましたが、事態の収束に伴い、再び国際色豊かな日常が戻ってくることでしょう。外国からの訪問客が増加すれば、日本固有の文化を説明・紹介する機会にも多く恵まれるはずです。英語という外国語を介して日本文化に触れることは、その独自性を再発見することにもつながるでしょう。本書の学習を通じて、英語で日本について発信する方法を身に付けて頂けることを願っております。

最後になりましたが、刊行にあたっては、日本英語表現学会の先生方から多くのご助言を頂きました。特に、企画からテキストの新しいアイデアに至るまで、吉田雅之先生から種々の刺激的なご提案を賜りました。辞書の使い方について山田茂先生から玉稿をお寄せ頂けたことも本書の華となりました。会長の藤本昌司先生からも、全体の統括面で色々とご示唆を頂戴いたしました。他にも学会員の先生方のお力添えがなければ、本書の内容を充実させることはできませんでした。さらに、株式会社南雲堂様にもこのような出版機会を頂き、編集段階でもご苦労を賜りました。この場を借りて厚く御礼申し上げます。

著者一同

2020 年盛夏

本書の特長

日本語のエッセイと英語のEssayは根本的に異なるものです。前者は、筆者の経験を読者と共有するために書かれた散文です。それに対して後者は、著者の主張に正当性があることを訴えて読者を説得するために書かれます。本書で使用するEssayという語は、日本語のエッセイとは明確に区別されます。

◎ 本書の目的

1. WritingやReadingに必要な語彙知識を固め、Essayの読み書きに応用できるようになること
2. Essay Writingの基礎を学び、段落構成の整った300語以上の英作文ができるようになること
3. Essayの構造を知り、Reading能力を高め、効率的に英文が読めるようになること

◎ WritingからReadingへ／ReadingからWritingへ

Essayには多くのルールやテクニックが存在します。それらを学習することでWritingの能力が飛躍的に向上するのはもちろん、Readingの能力も高めることが期待できます。Writingの教科書として使用する場合は、各Unitに収録されたEssayを英作文の具体例に見立てることができます。一方、Readingの教材として利用する場合は、その読解のために必要なルールやテクニックをWriting Sectionの解説や設問からも確認することができます。

◎ すべては読み手のために

Essayには読者が読みやすいように様々な工夫が施されています。日本語の文章を翻訳機にかけて完成というわけではないのです。本書では「どのようにすれば読みやすい文章が書けるのか」に焦点を当てています。読みやすさのために必要な要素は主に次の3点に集約されます。

1. 客観性……主観的表現を排除する、データや具体例で根拠を示す
2. 一貫性……話題を絞る、段落構成を整える、文と文の繋がりを作る
3. 経済性……同じ内容なら短い文を使う、複文よりも単文を使う

これらを組み入れることで、読み手の関心を惹き付けるようなEssayを書くことができます。主観的な表現を排除し、客観的でわかりやすい文章を書くためには、文法の正確さに加えて、語彙に含まれる様々な情報も理解しておかなければなりません。「類語」や「上位概念と下位概念」などを用いて表現に幅を持たせ、読み手に飽きられない工夫をしましょう。さらに、同じ意味をもった別の表現に書き換えられれば、文の繋がりが滑らかになり、より読者に伝わりやすい文章になります。

本書では、「日本に興味のある外国人留学生」を読者と仮定し、以上のようなポイントをおさえながら効果的なEssayの書き方（読み方）を考えていきます。

◎ 本書の構成

上記で示した3点を習得していくために、本書は以下のような構成になっています。

Unit	内容	主な学習項目
1~3	Essay全体で求められるもの	・三人称のみで表現する ・3つの文の繋がりを意識する

4~9	Essay の中心となる部分	・本論の基本的構造と展開方法を把握する ・短く簡潔な文で表現する
10~12	Essay をより読みやすくする部分	・序論と結論の構造及びその役割を把握する ・法助動詞を適切に活用する
13~15	応用と実践	・抽象性の高い内容を表現する ・より長い英作文に挑戦する

各 Unit は次のように構成されています。

[Vocabulary]

各 Unit のテーマに関わる写真が 6 枚提示されています。これらから連想される言葉を思いつく限り書いていきます。写真に写っているものだけでなく、それらの同義語や類義語、上位概念と下位概念に関する語までもおさえると、語彙の幅が広がり効果的な Writing や Reading につながっていきます。解答欄には名詞・動詞・形容詞・副詞という品詞の区分を設けています。これらの分類を意識することも文章を構築するうえでは重要です。品詞がわからない場合は辞書を使って調べましょう。

[Pre-writing]

「Vocabulary」で学習した語彙を用いて、文を作成します。これ以降のセクションに登場する語彙もここで確認しておきましょう。

[Drop-by]

コラムです。その Unit で扱っている Topic に関連する様々な語彙や背景について紹介しています。

[Grammar]

各 Unit で中心的に扱う文法項目や、Essay Writing に必要な規則や技術を学習します。

[Writing Task 1]

「Vocabulary」や「Pre-writing」において学習した表現を中心とし、その Unit のテーマに沿った語句や文を一段落分の長さに相当する文章で確認していきます。日本語の自然な言い回しを、英語ではどのように言い換えているか、文と文のつながりを良くするために、どのような工夫がされているか、それらを見極めるのも学習のポイントです。

[Writing Task 2]

Essay Writing に欠かせない技術や知識を紹介する箇所です。Unit ごとに異なる様々な問題を解きながら、それらを身につけていきます。

[Writing Task 3]

応用問題、あるいは発展的な課題です。Writing 中心の授業、または習熟度の高い学習者向けです。

[Reading Task]

その Unit のテーマに沿った Essay の一例です。内容理解のための問題を解きながら、Essay Writing の基礎も確認できるようになっています。Essay 全体の内容ももちろんですが、その細部において読み手のためにどのような工夫が施されているかにも注目しながら読んでみましょう。

辞書の使い方（1）

山田　茂

はじめに

アウトップを意識したインプットを！―辞書こそが最強のツール

安易に翻訳サイトなどに頼らず、是非、辞書（紙、電子、ウェブ、アプリ）を使ってほしい。なぜか？現在の辞書は、コーパス（言語のビッグデータ）に基づき、プロにより編集、執筆されているので、内容が信頼できる。意味のみならず、発音、文法、語法、語源、挿絵もワンストップで示してくれる。電子辞書では、これらの情報に縦横無尽にアクセスできる。意味を調べるだけではもったいない！文法、コロケーション、例文もチェックし、発信に使える情報、表現をどんどんインプットしていってほしい。その積み重ねが、英語を適切に話し、書けることにつながる。辞書の使い方(1)および(2)では、受信（読解)、発信（作文）のための英語辞書の使い方のポイントを解説する。外国人学習者向けの学習英英辞典も扱う。

受信(読解)のための辞書の使い方

英和辞典と英英辞典

下の embrace の意味は「抱擁する」ではない。英和辞典と英英辞典でチェックしてみよう。

> They eventually embraced an appearance featuring extremely tanned skin with wide white eyeliner and lipstick, a style known by the name *yamanba-gyaru* (monstrous gals)（本書 p. 54, l. 22）.

⁺**em·brace** /ɪmbréɪs, em-/
一[動] (**em•brac•es** /~ɪz/; **em•braced** /~t/; **em•brac•ing**) (他)
1 〈…〉を**抱き締める**, 抱擁する (hug).
·The mother *embraced* her child. その母親は子供を抱き締めた.
2 《格式》〈申し出など〉を喜んで受ける (accept).
3 《格式》〈主義・信仰など〉を奉ずる, いだく, 信ずる.
4 [進行形なし] 《格式》〈…〉を含む, 包含する (include) 《☞all-embracing》.
一(自) **抱き合う**.
·They shook hands and *embraced*. 彼らは握手して抱き合った.
【語源】古(期)フランス語で「両腕《☞brace【語源】》の中へ《☞em-》」の意.
一[名] (**em•brac•es** /~ɪz/)
1 [C] **抱擁**.
·in a close *embrace* しっかりと抱き合って.
2 [単数形で] (申し出などの)受け入れ; (主義などの)信奉.

2. VERB

If you embrace a change, political system, or idea, you accept it and start supporting it or believing in it.

[*formal*]

He embraces the new information age. [VERB noun]
The new rules have been embraced by government watchdog organizations. [be VERB-ed]

Synonyms: accept, support, receive, welcome　More Synonyms of embrace

それぞれの辞書の2番目の語義「受け入れる」が該当することがわかる。英英の定義を訳すと以下のようになる：

> If you **embrace** a change, political system, or idea, you accept it and start supporting it or believing in it.
> もしあなたが変化や政治制度や考えを embrace するのであれば、あなたはそれを受け入れ、それを支持または信奉し始める。

文定義は、if 節が見出し語の使い方を、主節が意味を示している。if 節は、embrace（「受け入れる」）が、主語に「人」、目的語に「変化、政治制度、考え」などを取る*他動詞であることを示している。

英和辞典は日本人に向けられており、わかりやすい。受信用の二言語辞書としては世界トップレベルにある。情報量（収録語、語義数）においては一般的に学習英英辞典を凌駕する。専門用語、固有名詞なども数多く収録されている（そもそも専門用語を英英辞典で引いてもピンとこない！）。

*どのような範疇の語と共に使われるか、どのような範疇の語に関して使われるかを「選択制限」という

辞書検索プロセス

辞書学の大家ハートマン教授（Hartmann 2001: 89-92）は、辞書検索を以下の7段階に分けている。普段何気なく行っている辞書検索だが、解説と注記を加えたので振り返ってみよう。

辞書検索プロセスの7段階	解　説	注　記
1. 問題の認識	わからない、しっくりこない表現があることを認識する	基本語の周辺的語義（意味）、成句がスルーされがちなので要注意
2. 問題となる語の特定	問題が起因する語句を特定する	電子辞書では、見出し語／成句／例文のいずれで引くかの決定が重要になる
3. 辞書の選択	問題を解決するために適切な辞書を選ぶ	電子辞書の「複数辞書検索」機能を使えば辞書を選ぶ必要はない
4. 見出し語の選択	（例えばイディオムなどは）どの見出し語の下に適切な情報が載っているかを決定する	電子辞書では、見出し語を完全に入力しなくても候補を示してくれる。「成句検索」では見出し語を特定する必要がない
5. 語義の選択	何番の意味の下に適切な情報が載っているかを決定する	英英辞典では語義がたくさんある項目には、サインポスト（意味の小見出し）が付加され、語義選択がしやすくなっている
6. 有用な情報の抽出	定義、訳語、例文、語法欄などを読み、問題解決に使える情報を採取する	英英辞典では、定義が2000～3000の基本語でなされ、定義文も導入され、定義がわかりやすくなっている
7. 情報の活用	辞書から得られた情報を活用し所期の問題の解決に役立てる	元の文と辞書との間を行きつ戻りつしながら問題を解決していくこともある

文法、品詞が重要！

上記検索プロセスの「4. 見出し語の選択」、「5. 語義の選択」において、文法、品詞の知識が重要となる。辞書は見出し語が品詞別に立てられており、各語義にも有用な文法情報が示されている。これらの情報は英文を組み立てる時のみならず、辞書の検索でもキーとなる。

下の文中の talks を『ルミナス英和辞典』で引いてみよう。

Trade talks are progressing well.

まずは「4. 見出し語の選択」だが、品詞は何か？ talks は talk の複数形で、名詞である。
次に「5. 語義の選択」だ。名詞の項目には 6 つの語義がエントリーされている。どの語義が該当するか？

一名 (**~s** /~s/)
1 🄲 **話, 談話**, 座談《☞speech 類義語》.
・We had a good ***talk about*** it. 私たちはそのことについてじっくりと話し合った.
・We had several *talks* ***with*** them *about* it. 私たちはそれについて彼らと数回話し合った.
2 🄲 (非公式の)**講話**, 講演 (speech); **講義**.
・give a ***talk to*** the students ***on*** [***about***] reading 学生に読書について(くだけた)話をする.
3 [複数形で] **会談**; **相談**; 協議.
・preliminary「peace *talks* [*talks* ***on*** peace] 和平交渉の予備会談[折衝].
・summit *talks* 首脳会談.
・I had many *talks* ***with*** the doctor ***about*** my boy. 息子のことで医者と何度も相談した.
4 [the ~] **話の種**, 話題; うわさの種; 🅄 うわさ.
・「He is [They are] ***the talk of*** the town. 彼[彼ら]は町中のうわさの的だ.
・**【言い換え】** There is a lot of ***talk of*** her go***ing*** to France next month. <N+*of*+動名>=There is a lot of ***talk that*** she is going to France next month. <N+*that* 節> 彼女が来月フランスへ行くといううわさでもちきりだ.
5 🅄 [普通は all [just] ~] Ⓢ 意味のない話, 口先だけのこと.
・That's *just* (a lot of) *talk*. それは単なる話の上のことにすぎない.
・She's *all talk* (and [but] no action). 彼女は口先ばかりだ.
6 🅄 [主に合成語で] 話し方, 口調.
・☞baby talk.

『ルミナス英和辞典』の talk の項目 © Kenkyusha Co., Ltd.

日本語の訳語をスキャンするのも悪くはないが、第一に注目すべきは、語義番号の直後に示されている文法的な表示、注記だ。🄲は可算、🅄は不可算を表す。Talks（複数形）なので、「3.［複数形で］」に目が留まる。訳語に「会談；相談；協議」とあり、元の文の意味に当てはまる。辞書の例文の訳語にも「（和平）交渉」、「（首脳）会談」とあるので、語義 3 が該当すると断定する。

「5. 語義の選択」は重要なステップである。以下のような情報を手掛かりに絞り込みを行い、クリアーしなければならない。また、似ている用例を探すという方法も有効である：

名詞：可算・不可算（🄲・🅄）[countable・uncountable]
動詞：自動詞・他動詞（🄸・🅃）[intransitive verb・transitive verb]
形容詞：限定用法・叙述用法（🄰・🄿）[attributive・predicative]
サインポスト（英英辞典の意味の小見出し）
定義／訳語
選択制限（p.7 参照）
太字（文法的パターン、成句を示す）

Contents

Unit 1

The Story of *Wagashi*

一人称・二人称を使わず客観的に書く

1
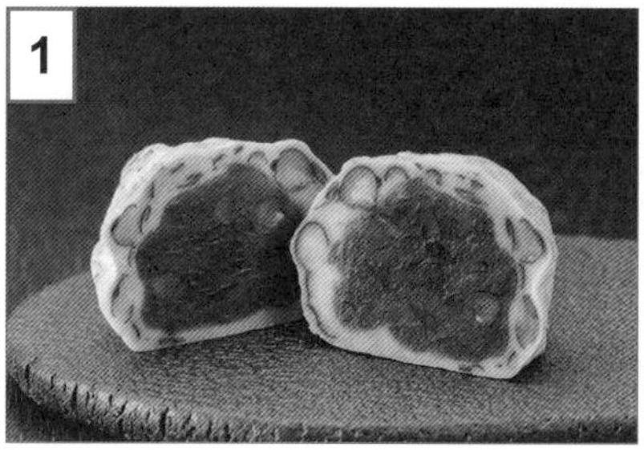

2

3

4

5

6

Vocabulary 上の写真を参考に、「和菓子」に関連しそうな語句を集め、表にまとめてみましょう。似たような意味を持つ語句を複数書いても構いません。

名詞／名詞相当表現	形容詞／形容詞相当表現	動詞／動詞相当表現	副詞／副詞相当表現
・tea	・delicate	・create	・widely
・sweets	・pretty	・produce	・gradually
・	・	・	・
・	・	・	・
・	・	・	・
・	・	・	・
・	・	・	・
・	・	・	・
・	・	・	・
・	・	・	・

Pre-Writing 〔　　〕内のヒントを参考に、英文を完成させましょう。(　　) には与えられた文字で始まる語が入ります。

1) Japanese confectionary (c 　　　　　) plant-based (i 　　　　　).
〔写真 1 より：日本の菓子は、植物性の材料でできている。〕

2) Plant-based ingredients (a 　　　　　) (u 　　　　　) to make Japanese sweets.
〔写真 1 より：日本の菓子は、植物性の材料でできている。〕

3) The prevalence of tea ceremonies (g 　　　　　) (d 　　　　　) Japanese confectionary.
〔写真 2 より：茶道の流行によって、和菓子は徐々に発展した。〕

4) To attract tourists to their region, artisans (c 　　　　　) (u 　　　　　) sweets.
〔地方への旅行者を惹きつけるために、職人たちは独特な菓子を造り出した。〕

5) Nowadays, some (l 　　　　　) traditional sweets such as *sakura-mochi* are (w 　　　　　) known throughout Japan.
〔桜餅のようないくつかの地方独特の伝統的な菓子は、現在では日本全体に広く知られている。〕

Drop-by

室町時代の末から江戸時代初期にかけて、オランダ、スペイン、ポルトガルからの宣教師たちが布教活動のために日本にやってきました。彼らがキリスト教とともに日本にもたらしたのが西洋のお菓子です。織田信長は宣教師から confetti を献上され、大変気に入ったと言われています。当時の日本では鶏卵やバターを使ったり、オーブンで焼き上げたりするような西洋の菓子に馴染みがありませんでした。それがキリスト教とともに徐々に広まり、その材料や製法が、日本の菓子作りにも応用されました。洋菓子の材料や製造法を和菓子に取り入れたものが「南蛮菓子」と呼ばれ、それぞれの菓子の名称も日本風に解釈されています。例えば「カステラ」はスペイン・カステーリャ王国のパン Bolo de Castella が語源で、英語では sponge cake に相当します。サクサクとした焼き菓子の「ぼうろ」と bolo の関連も見られますが、英語では biscuit と言います。金平糖は英語の confect、イタリア語の confetti、ポルトガル語の confeitos など糖菓を表すものを語源としています。金平糖は伝来当初、製造方法が秘密とされていましたが、日本の菓子職人の工夫によって今のとげのある形になりました。

Grammar

次に示す文章は、一人称・二人称を主語として書かれています。これは主観的になるだけではなく、主語が何(誰)を指すのか分かりにくい文にしてしまいます。Essayでは一人称・二人称を主語にせず、客観的な視点で書くと説得力が増します。主語を変えて下線部を補い、より客観的な文にしてみましょう。

1) We send a variety of *wagashi* as a gift on special occasions.
   A variety of *wagashi* is ______________________________ on special occasions.

2) We were not yet familiar with European sweets at that time.
   ______________________________ were not yet familiar to Japanese people at that time.

3) You use only plant-based ingredients to make traditional *wagashi*.
   Traditional *wagashi* ______________________________ only plant-based ingredients.

4) I think sweet red bean paste, *anko*, is popular with many elderly people.
   ______________________________ are fond of sweet red bean paste: *anko*.

Writing Task 1

次の日本文に合うように、英文中の空欄を埋めてみましょう。日本文では能動態でも、英文では受動態になっている文もあります。なお、(　　) には与えられた文字で始まる語が入ります。

和菓子は日本の歴史の中で変化してきました。外国の文化や宗教の流入がその発展に影響を与えてきたのです。例えば、揚げる、蒸すなどの調理法は禅僧たちが中国から持ち帰ったものです。西洋の宣教師たちは、たくさんの砂糖や卵が使われている洋菓子を携えて日本にやってきました。オーブンの使用も当時の日本の人々にとっては新しいものでした。職人たちはこれらの新しい調理方法や材料を徐々に応用し、様々な独特の和菓子を創り出していきました。

Japanese confectionary has [1] (c　　　　　) throughout Japanese history. The introduction of foreign [2] (c　　　　　) and religions has [3] (i　　　　　) its development. For instance, cooking techniques such as frying and [4] (s　　　　　) were brought from China by Zen monks. European missionaries came to Japan with their sweets containing a lot of white [5] (s　　　　　) and eggs. The [6] (u　　　　　) of ovens was also new to Japanese people at that time. New cooking [7] (m　　　　　) and ingredients were gradually adopted to Japanese confectionary by artisans, who soon invented a [8] (v　　　　　) of unique creations.

Writing Task 2

Essay Writing とは日本語でいう随筆ではなく、論理的・客観的な文章を書くことです。客観的な文章を英語で書くためには、まず著者の主観を排除する必要があり、以下の点が重要です。

1. 【一人称・二人称を使わない：I , we , you などを主語とした主観の入る文は避ける】

   例 1：I think that Ghibli movies are touching.

   （× 著者個人の意見になってしまう）

2. 【あいまいな表現を使わない：主観的な形容詞や副詞の使用は避けるか、補足する】

   例 2：Many people say that Japanese train operation is punctual.

   （× 具体的に何人から many people とするかは人によって判断が異なる）

3. 【法助動詞を使わない：can , must , should , may , will 等には著者の主観が入るので避ける】

   例 3：Everyone can experience tea ceremonies in Kyoto.

   （× 体験できると思う、という著者の主観的判断であり、客観的事実を述べた文ではない）

では、次の英文を指示に従ってより客観的になるよう書き換えてみましょう。

1) The city of Kyoto has many temples.（「1700 以上の」という具体的な数字を加えて）

   The city of Kyoto has (　　　　　) (　　　　　) (　　　　　) temples.

2) For many people, sweets will be very good souvenirs.（法助動詞を使わず、曖昧さを除いて）

   For people who love the tea ceremony, sweets (　　　　　) very good souvenirs.

3) I read that there are many Western people who drink green tea with honey.（主語を変えて）

   (　　　　　) (　　　　　) the magazine, some Western people drink green tea with honey.

4) Everyone knows that Japanese train operation is punctual.（主語を変えて）

   Japanese trains are famous for (　　　　　) (　　　　　).

Writing Task 3

日本の有名な食べ物を一・二人称や法助動詞を使わず客観的に三文程度で説明してみましょう。

例）どら焼き　大福もち　ひなあられ

The Story of *Wagashi*

Due to its global recognition, sushi is a commonly known example of a typical traditional Japanese food. For people in Japan, however, “traditional” means not just what is popular worldwide but what has been developed throughout the history of Japanese eating habits, religions, and economy. One of the greatest examples is *wagashi* (和菓子).

Wagashi — a combination of *wa* (和 “Japanese”) and *gashi* (=*kashi*; 菓子 “confection”) — represents Japanese dietary culture well. *Kashi* were served with meals in ancient times and originally made only from plant-based ingredients such as fruit or nuts. Later, people started to process rice and wheat containing sweet malt to make foodstuffs like *mochi* and *dango*. In the 6th century, *amazura* syrup extracted from ivy plants was used as a sweetener. Since the extraction procedure was complex, it was quite precious and only consumed by aristocrats.

The introduction of foreign religions had a great effect on the evolution of *wagashi*. In the 7th century, Zen monks returning from China brought back tea drinking customs and *Kara-gashi*, Chinese confections. Zen-influenced culture expanded the need in Japan for sweets to be served with tea and for the development of some new *wagashi* cooking techniques such as frying and steaming. These were gradually applied to Japanese confections like *karinto* and *manju*.

In the 17th century, the stable economy allowed *wagashi* to become dramatically more elaborate. In this period of peace, the prevalence of tea ceremonies raised the demand for attractive sweets to delight guests. Commoners also started to enjoy leisure travel to temples, shrines, and hot springs. Near these tourist spots, local merchants soon appeared. They competed with each other to produce unique and beautiful confections to attract visitors. To be selected by customers, something simple like *mochi* was polished into sophisticated creations, for example, *sakura-mochi* and *kusa-mochi*, by skilled artisans. They had their own distinctive styles and their cooking methods were handed down over the generations.

Wagashi is a food developed throughout Japanese history. Ultimately, it has reached the point where people inevitably appreciate and feel its exotic charm.

---

come to mind: 思い浮かぶ　recognition: 認知　ingredient: 材料　plant-based: 植物性の
process: 加工する　sweet malt : 麦芽糖　ivy plant: ツル性植物　extract: 抽出する　aristocrats : 貴族
confectionary: 菓子　elaborate: 精巧な　prevalence: 普及・流行　artisan: 職人　hand down: 受け継ぐ
sophisticated: 洗練された　distinctive: 特有の　inevitably: せずにはいられない

1. 和菓子の “plant-based ingredients” の例として挙げられているものを２段落目からすべて抜き出しましょう。

例）fruit, nuts

2. *“kashi”* の言い換えとして用いられている名詞や名詞句を本文中からすべて抜き出しましょう。

3. 本文中で述べられていないものは次のうちどれでしょうか。

a. The development of *wagashi* was influenced by some foreign cultures.

b. Tea drinking customs had expanded the consumption of *wagashi*.

c. *Wagashi* rapidly spread all over Japan in the 7th century.

d. The 17th century is the period of prosperity that accelerated the growth of Japanese confections.

e. Using natural ingredients is one of the features of Japanese sweets.

4. 本文の内容をもとに、(　　) に指定された頭文字で始まる語を入れましょう。原則として本文中で使用されている単語が入りますが、必要に応じて形を変えましょう。

1) *Kashi* (r　　　　　) eating habits in Japan well.

2) *Amazura* syrup is an ancient sweetener which is (e　　　　　) (f　　　　　) ivy plants.

3) Unique types of *wagashi* were (d　　　　　) (d　　　　　) around the 17th century.

4) Modern-day *wagashi* is created as the result of the (c　　　　　) among skilled (a　　　　　) to attract customers.

5. 本文に関する次の英文をより客観的な文になるように書き換えてみましょう。

1) Many visitors must be attracted by the beauty of Japanese sweets.

2) I think that many people will eat *tsukimi dango* on the night of harvest moon.

Unit 2

Architecture: Japanese Castles

文の繋がりを意識する

1

2

3

4

5

6

Vocabulary 上の写真を参考に、「城」に関連しそうな語句を集め、表にまとめてみましょう。似たような意味を持つ語句を複数書いても構いません。

名詞／名詞相当表現	形容詞／形容詞相当表現	動詞／動詞相当表現	副詞／副詞相当表現
・timber	・unique	・construct	・strongly
・wood	・typical	・function	・masterfully
・	・	・	・
・	・	・	・
・	・	・	・
・	・	・	・
・	・	・	・
・	・	・	・
・	・	・	・
・	・	・	・

Pre-Writing

〔　　〕内のヒントを参考に、英文を完成させましょう。（　　）には与えられた文字で始まる語が入ります。

1) Japanese castles are (w　　　　　　) for their (u　　　　　　) appearance.
〔写真 1 より：日本の城はその独特の外観で有名だ。〕

2) Their distinctive appearance (m　　　　　　) Japanese castles (f　　　　　　).
〔写真 1 より：日本の城はその独特の外観で有名だ。〕

3) Castles (b　　　　　　) in flatlands are often (s　　　　　　) by a moat called *o-hori*.
〔写真 2 より：平地に建てられた城は、しばしばお堀によって囲まれている。〕

4) In Japanese history, castles (f　　　　　　) as a (f　　　　　　) in battles.
〔日本の歴史の中で、城は戦いの際に要塞として機能した。〕

5) In ancient times, (m　　　　　　) for most European buildings were stones. They are (e　　　　　　) to work than Japanese ones.
〔昔、主なヨーロッパの建物の材料は石材だった。それらは日本のもの（石材）よりも加工しやすい。〕

Drop-by

日本の城といって思い浮かべるのは、その象徴と言える天守（天守閣）のことでしょう。天守は日本独自のものですが、英語ではその役割から keep とあらわされます。海外の多くの城は天守の代わりに窓の付いた石造りの塔（tower）を持ちます。ロンドン塔（Tower of London）などはその代表例です。一方、日本の天守は白い壁（clay walls）と瓦でできた三角形の破風（gables）が特徴です。瓦屋根の上には装飾があり、名古屋城名物、左右対になった金のしゃちほこはその姿から Golden Dolphins と訳されます。白壁に開いた三角や四角の穴は狭間（arrow slits）と呼ばれ、そこから弓矢や鉄砲を撃ち敵の侵入を阻みました。城の敷地内には見張りのための木造の櫓（watch tower）が置かれ、木や芝生の植えられた中庭（baileys）や小川や池のある日本庭園（Japanese gardens）、茶道のための茶室（tea house, tea room）などが見られます。そのような城や天守は、明治時代の「廃城令」（the ordiance abolishing castles）、戦時中の空襲、自然災害での倒壊や焼失などにより多くが失われてしまいました。江戸時代以前に築城され、現在も残っている天守はたった 12 しかありません。貴重な当時の姿とその内部に凝らされた建築的な工夫を見に、全国の現存十二天守（The 12 Castles with Existing Castle Towers）を訪ねてみてはどうでしょうか。

Grammar

英文では同じ単語を繰り返し使うことは好まれません。くどくて稚拙な印象を読者に与えてしまうからです。次の英文の下線部を代名詞や類語、あるいは上位語（例：dog の場合は animal）に置き換えて単語の重複をなくし、文のつながりが良くなるよう書き換えましょう。

1) One popular kind of health resort is *onsen*.
Onsen became more accessible to ordinary people in the 17th century. (　　　　　　)
This is because ordinary people gradually became more prosperous. (　　　　　　)

2) Himeji-jo is the most well-known castle in Hyogo prefecture.
Millions of tourists visit Hyogo prefecture to see the structure. (　　　　　　)
Himeji-jo is likened to *shirasagi* (a white egret) due to Himeji-jo's beauty.
(　　　　　　/　　　　　　)

3) European missionaries introduced Western cake to Japan.
Eggs are an essential ingredient for baking Western cake. (　　　　　　)
However, eggs were not initially familiar to Japanese people as ingredients for confectionary. (　　　　　　/　　　　　　)

Writing Task 1

次の日本文に合うように、英文中の空欄を埋めてみましょう。なお、(　　) には与えられた文字で始まる語が入ります。

海外の古くて有名な建築物には、レンガや石材で作られているものがたくさんあります。たとえば中世ヨーロッパのお城や寺院、中国の万里の長城などです。それらは何世紀も外観を留めるほどに強靭です。一方で、古来の和風建築には木が多く使われています。それは日本の地形的特徴や頻発する地震のような自然災害のためです。木造の建物は地震に対して強いので、木材が主な建築材料として使用されました。しかし、木材にも弱点があります。火事です。沖縄の首里城のように火事のために失われた古い建物がたくさんありました。

Famous architectural structures [1](m　　　　　) of stones and bricks are still preserved abroad. For instance, there are medieval castles and cathedrals in Europe and the Great Wall of China. [2](T　　　　　) are strong enough to last for centuries. On the other hand, [3](w　　　　　) was used to build most Japanese old architectural structures. [4](T　　　　　) is due to Japanese natural [5](d　　　　　) and land features. Japan experiences frequent [6](e　　　　　). Wooden buildings are resistant to tremors, so timbers were used as the primary building material. However, wood has a [7](d　　　　　): fires. There is much old architecture which has been [8](l　　　　　) to flame, like Shuri-jo in Okinawa.

Writing Task 2

英文では、いくつかの文章からなるまとまりのある paragraph を書く際に注意点として　A）同じ語の繰り返しを避けるため、他の語（代名詞や類語）で置き換える　B）流れを考えて文の順序を整える　という 2 つのポイントが上げられます。例を見てみましょう。

One of the most famous tourism spots in Kyoto is ***Kiyomizu-dera***.

It is best known for its **high wooden stage** built in the 8th century.

At that time, **the platform** was constructed without using any screws.

京都で最も有名な観光地の一つが清水寺です。

それは 8 世紀に建てられた、高い木造の舞台があることで最も知られています。

当時、その舞台を建てるのに釘は一切使われていないのです。

○ 同じ語を 2 回目に使うときは　代名詞に変える　*Kiyomizu-dera* → it

類語に変える　built → constructed

別の言い方に変える　high wooden stage → the platform

8th century → at that time

○ 大まかな話題の紹介から始め、その細かい説明をしていく

以上の点に留意し、まとまりのある 3 文の paragraph になるように、3 つの文を並べかえて（　　）に順番を書き入れましょう。

1) These openings are for shooting arrows without exposing oneself to enemies. (　　)

Some of them have triangular holes on their walls.　(　　)

In ancient times, castles were often used as fortresses. (　　)

2) The event is called *yuki matsuri*, the festival of snow and ice.　(　　)

As its name *yuki* indicates, the show takes place in the snowy season. (　　)

Sapporo holds a very famous seasonal exhibition. (　　)

Writing Task 3

Writing Task 2 の A）と B）の点に注意し、日本特有のものについて 3 文で説明する英文を作ってみましょう。

例）瀬戸物　こけし　提灯　南部鉄器　だるま

Architecture: Japanese Castles

Castles are impressive structures constructed from various materials in various styles. For example, the World Heritage site of the Historic Fortified City of Carcassonne in France has a castle and surrounding ramparts constructed with stones. Meanwhile, Japanese castles are known for ① their unique features. What makes them such special structures?

Building materials are the most prominent feature. The majority of castles in Japan have a solid stone foundation. This allows the buildings to stand on complicated geography including hills and rivers. However, using stones for entire structures was dangerous because of the potential for collapse triggered by Japan's frequent earthquakes (approximately ten percent of all earthquakes worldwide). This situation requires more flexible and easily available materials for building elements such as timbers for pillars, floors, and ceilings. Wooden buildings have good resistance to earthquakes but poor to fire. Therefore, fireproof elements like *shikkui* plaster are used for outer walls and *kawara* tiles for roofs.

The location of castles is also a notable characteristic. They were usually constructed on the top of hills in the 15th century. At that time, the central government's power declined and all of Japan was experiencing territorial disputes between warring states. To defend against invaders, castles assumed the function of fortress. For that purpose, higher ground proved expedient and these castles came to be called *yama-shiro* (山城, mountain castles), of which Bicchu-Matsuyama-jo is a typical example. Once the confusion of the territorial dispute period had passed, castles gradually lost their role as fortress and started to be constructed in flatland areas. These are called *hira-shiro* (平城, flatland castles). ② They focused on governance of the castle towns, *joka-machi*. To protect a castle or whole city against unexpected invaders, surrounding moats called *o-hori* were dug. One of the most famous examples of this is Osaka-jo.

Materials and location made Japanese castles different from ③ those in other countries. Some of the older Japanese castles are still standing, but ④ others were destroyed in wars and natural disasters such as earthquakes and fires, like Kumamoto-jo and Shuri-jo. Some of them were rebuilt as symbols of recovery. Whether castles are the original structure or reconstructed, they remind the present generation of how people lived in the past.

Historic Fortified City of Carcassonne: 歴史的城塞都市カルカソンヌ　ramparts: 城壁
potential: 可能性のある　collapse: 崩落　fireproof: 耐火性の　warring: 交戦中の　invader: 侵略者
fortress: 要塞　expedient: 好都合の　the territorial dispute period: 戦国時代

1. “castle” の言い換えとして用いられている名詞や名詞句を本文中からすべて抜き出しましょう。

2. 本文中の下線部① ～ ④が指すものを書きましょう。

① their ( ) ② They ( )
③ those ( ) ④ others ( )

3. ２段落目の日本の城の建築材料の特色をまとめた英文です。同じ語の繰り返しを避けるため、下線部の語を別の言い方に変えて（ ）に入れ、英文を完成させましょう。

Wood and *shikkui* plaster were used to build Japanese castles in the 15th century . These ( ) are ideal to ( ) structures which have superior earthquake resistance. ( ) is necessary for Japanese buildings due to frequent ( ).

4. 本文中で述べられていないものは次のうちどれでしょうか。２つ選びましょう。

a. Building materials are one of the features that makes Japanese castles unique.
b. There have been many earthquakes in Japanese history.
c. Japanese castles have moats around them so that they acquire good transportation.
d. Bicchu-Matsuyama-jo is a typical example of a *yama-shiro*.
e. The quality of Japanese stones is suitable to build the main buildings of castles.

5. 本文に使われている語で、（ ）に示されている文字で始まる語を入れて、要約文を完成させましょう。ただし、本文の語の品詞を変える必要のある箇所もあります。

Japanese castles have an unique architectural style. One [1](f) is their building [2](m). Unlike castles in other countries, [3](t) were used extensively. Japanese [4](s) were inappropriate for entire buildings due to the potential collapse by earthquakes. As a [5](f), *yama-shiro* were built on the top of mountains. After the wars, when peace came, more castles began to be constructed on [6](f) for efficient [7](g). It resulted in an economical flourish of the castle [8](t). These are major [9](c) of Japanese castles. They remind the current generation of the [10](l) of people in the past.

Matsuri : Festivals in Japan

ほぼ同じ意味を持つ別の表現を考えてみる

1

2

3

4

5

6

Vocabulary 上の写真を参考に、「祭り」に関連しそうな語句を集め、表にまとめてみましょう。似たような意味を持つ語句を複数書いても構いません。

名詞／名詞相当表現	形容詞／形容詞相当表現	動詞／動詞相当表現	副詞／副詞相当表現
・line	・local	・queue	・actually
・crowd	・ritual	・mourn	・excitingly
・	・	・	・
・	・	・	・
・	・	・	・
・	・	・	・
・	・	・	・
・	・	・	・
・	・	・	・
・	・	・	・

Pre-Writing 〔　　〕内のヒントを参考に、英文を完成させましょう。(　　) には与えられた文字で始まる語が入ります。

1) *Mikoshi* is a portable (s　　　　　　) carried by (l　　　　　　) people in a parade.
〔写真 1 より：神輿は、地元の人々が肩に担いでねりあるく小さな神社だ。〕

2) *Mikoshi* is a (r　　　　　　) of shrine (s　　　　　　) like a throne.
〔写真 1 より：神輿は神社を模した物で、王座の形に作られている。〕

3) Looking around the food (s　　　　　　) is a (f　　　　　　) part of Japanese festivals.
〔写真 2 より：露店を見て回るのは日本の祭りの楽しみのひとつだ。〕

4) In some seaside towns, *mikoshi* are carried into the sea to (p　　　　　　) the bodies and (s　　　　　　) of fishermen.
〔海辺の町では、漁師たちの心身を清めるために神輿を海の中まで担ぎ込むこともある。〕

5) Lots of (d　　　　　　) in unique costumes (p　　　　　　) in the Awa-odori festival in Tokushima.
〔徳島県の阿波踊りでは、独特の衣装を身に着けたたくさんの踊り手たちが舞い踊る。〕

Drop-by

祭りや盆踊りと並んで日本の夏に欠かせないもののひとつに花火があります。花火全般を fireworks と言いますが、打ち上げ花火は skyrockets、線香花火は sparklers、ねずみ花火は pinwheels などさまざまな種類のものが楽しまれています。大きな花火大会では約 4 万発もの花火が打ち上げられ、海外からも多くの見物客を集めます。一方、他国では花火の季節は夏だけではありません。イギリスでは 11 月の Guy Fawkes Day にロンドン中の公園で花火が打ち上げられます。また欧州各国では New Year's Eve などで冬の花火が見られます。Japan HANABI Association によれば、日本の打上花火の特徴は大きく 3 つ、① Seating「玉の座り」② Exploded diameter and symmetry「盆と肩」③ Lighting and disappearing timing「消え口」。「玉の座りが良い」花火は、開花が最も高く上がった瞬間に合ったもの、想定された最大直径で開花したものを「盆が良い」、開花の中心からの放射が真円になったものを「肩が広い」と評価します。また花火が消えるとき、光が一斉に同じタイミングで消えるものを「消え口が良い」と言うそうです。花火職人が何世代にもわたり作り上げたこの日本の花火の見どころを、ぜひ海外から来た人たちに紹介してみてください。

Grammar まとまった量の Essay を書く際に表現が単調にならないよう、一つの事象であっても別の言い回しを用いて表すことがあります。主語や文型を変えたりする手法が好例です。(　　) に与えられた文字で始まる語を入れて、日本語を説明する英文を何通りか作ってみましょう。

1) A person's first visit of a year to a shrine or a temple is called *hatsumoude* in Japanese.
神社かお寺への一年で最初のお参りを日本語で初詣といいます。

→ (V　　　　　) a shrine or a temple for the first (t　　　　　) in a year is *hatsumoude* in Japanese.

→ *Hatsumoude* is the Japanese word which means (m　　　　　) the first annual (v　　　　　) to a shrine or a temple.

2) *Hanabi taikai*, or fireworks displays, are events which are held throughout Japan during the summer.
花火大会は夏の時期に日本中で開催される行事です。

→ Fireworks displays, *hanabi taikai*, are (h　　　　　) in hundreds of (p　　　　　) in Japan mainly in the summer season.

→ In (s　　　　　), hundreds of *hanabi taikai*, or fireworks displays, are seen all (o　　　　　) Japan.

Writing Task 1 次の日本文に合うように、英文中の空欄を埋めてみましょう。なお、(　　) には与えられた文字で始まる語が入ります。

日本では、地方で行われる祭りの多くは夏から秋にかけて催されます。それは主に祭りが豊作を祈るための行事だからです。また、この時節は農業の中休みの時期と考えられています。だから祭りは忙しい農家の人々が、稲やその他の農作物の収穫の前につかの間の休息をとる良い理由なのです。お盆も八月の中旬、通常は 13 日から 16 日に催される大きな行事です。祖先の霊が、家族のもとに戻ってくると信じられています。彼らを迎えるために、各家庭では家を掃除し、仏壇の前に様々なお供え物を置きます。そのあと、家族のお墓参りをして祖先の霊を家に迎え入れるのです。霊を迎えたり、送り返したりするためのかがり火をたく家庭もあります。お盆は一年の中で最も長い休暇のひとつであり、家族が集まる良い機会でもあるのです。

In Japan, many local *matsuri*, Japanese festivals, are [1](h　　　　　) during summer and autumn months. It is this time of year mainly because *matsuri* are events where people [2](p　　　　　) to celebrate a good harvest. Also, this season is supposed to be an intermission of [3](a　　　　　) work. So *matsuri* are a good excuse for busy farmers to take a short [4](b　　　　　) before harvesting rice and other farm [5](p　　　　　). The *obon* period is also a big event that occurs in mid-August, usually from the 13th to the 16th. It is believed that the spirits of ancestors return to their homes during *obon*. To [6](w　　　　　) them, each family cleans their house and prepares a variety of offerings in front of their *butsudan*, a Buddhist altar. After that, they [7](v　　　　　) the grave to invite the spirits. To welcome and send off their ancestors, some people light ceremonial bonfires. *Obon* is one of the longest vacations of the year and a good [8](o　　　　　) for family gatherings.

Writing Task 2

Essay Writing では、同じ語の繰り返しを避けるために代名詞・類語等で置き換えることを前 Unit で学びました。さらに、似たような表現の繰り返しで文の流れが単調になるのを避けるため、類語や上位概念を表す語句によって言い回しを変えることがあります。例として下線部分の繰り返しを類語や上位概念を表す語句に置き換えてみます。Unit 2 の内容を例にみてみましょう。

Japanese castles are unique. Japanese castles are unique because Japanese castles are made of wood and *shikkui* plaster. To use wood and *shikkui* plaster for castles is unique. Foreign tourists come to see Japanese castles.

Japanese castles are unique. This is because the main buildings are made of wood and *shikkui* plaster. Using these building materials for castles is unusual, so overseas visitors come to see the architecture.

類語・上位語への置き換え

Japanese castles ⇒ the main building, the architecture

wood and *shikkui* plaster ⇒ these building materials

例を参考に、次の英文をつながりが良く読みやすくなるように別の言い回しなどに書き換えてみましょう。

1) 下線部の語は繰り返し使用されています。代名詞、類語、上位語などに変えましょう。

Commoners started to enjoy leisure travel to temples, shrines, and hot springs. Near temples, shrines, and hot springs, local food shops soon appeared. Local food shops competed with each other to produce unique and beautiful confectionaries to attract tourists. Some of the famous unique and beautiful confectionaries are still popular.

→ Commoners started to enjoy leisure travel to temples, shrines, and hot springs. Near ______________, local food shops soon appeared. ______________ competed with each other to create unique and beautiful confectionaries to attract ______________. Some of the famous ______________ are still popular.

2) 下線部の語は繰り返し使用されています。他の語に置き換えたり、二文を一文にまとめたりして、繰り返しのない文にしてみましょう。

Japan has some famous festivals. One of the famous festivals is the Sapporo Snow Festival. Every year, lots of Japanese people visit Sapporo to see the famous festival. Lots of foreign people visit Sapporo, too.

Writing Task 3

日本のお祭りをひとつ取り上げ、3～4文の英文で説明してみましょう。その際、法助動詞や一人称、二人称の代名詞を使用しないようにし、文と文のつながりにも注意しましょう。

Matsuri : Festivals in Japan

In Japan, nearly 300,000 *matsuri* festivals are held annually, particularly during the summer and autumn months. The roots of the events are in Shinto or Buddhist rituals to celebrate the harvest, or in ceremonies to ward off disease and evil spirits. With the passage of time, they have transformed into events for ordinary people, which include various entertainments like food stalls. Above all, *mikoshi* and *bon-odori* have become ① two essential elements of *matsuri*.

Mikoshi is one of the most familiar parts of *matsuri*. It is a small replica of a Shinto shrine that is portable and is used as a vehicle to transport a god or goddess around during a festival. The participants carry the sacred litter on their shoulders and call out the cadence with phrases such as "*Wasshoi*!" to maintain their rhythm and momentum. Through such rituals, the locals invite a Shinto deity to inspect the area. The highlight of such events is different from region to region. In Aomori, there is a unique festival called Nebuta Matsuri, where the *mikoshi* is followed by about 20 large floats called ② *dashi*. They are beautifully decorated with approximately five-meter tall and nine-meter wide lanterns of mystical creatures and heroes. Meanwhile, in some seaside towns, *mikoshi* are shaken up and down as if they were riding the waves of the sea. During the Hamaori-sai in Kanagawa, 40 of them are actually carried into the sea one after another to purify the bodies and spirits of fishermen.

③ *Bon-odori* is rich in regional flavor. It is a local dance with traditional music performed by people dressed in *yukata*, a light cotton kimono. *Bon* is a summer event in August with some cultural similarities to Halloween in Western countries. People believe that ancestral spirits return to their families during this period. *Odori* means dance, which varies depending on the region. In local *bon-odori*, participants gather at nearby shrines or parks and dance to welcome the spirits. One of Japan's largest *bon-odori* events is annually held in Tokushima, ④ the Awa-odori festival. Nearly 10,000 dancers in unique hats and costumes perform in several teams, and the streets become full of spectators from within the country and abroad.

Nowadays, Japanese *matsuri* attracts not only Japanese people, but also foreign people. To truly understand the exciting energy of Japanese *matsuri*, people must simply experience one for themselves.

---

ward off : 避ける・防ぐ　　sacred: 神聖な　　litter: 輿（こし）　　cadence: 拍子・抑揚　　momentum : 勢い
deity: 神　　mystical: 神話上の・伝説上の　　purify : 清める

1. 第２段落の中から、*"mikoshi"* の言い換えとして用いられている名詞や名詞句をすべて抜き出しましょう。

2. 下線部①～④が指すものを、本文から抜き出して答えましょう。

① two essential elements (　　　　)

② *dashi* (　　　　)

③ *Bon-odori* (　　　　)

④ the Awa-odori festival (　　　　)

3. 本文中で述べられていないものは次のうちどれでしょうか。２つ選びましょう。

a. *Mikoshi* and *bon-odori* are often seen in Japanese festivals, *matsuri.*
b. Nebuta Matsuri has a large-scale parade of dancers in unique costumes.
c. The roots of Japanese *matsuri* are rituals to welcome diseases and evil spirits.
d. There are people from abroad who visit Japan to view *matsuri.*
e. *Bon-odori* originally existed to welcome ancestral spirits.

4. 最後の段落には語の繰り返しがあります。波線部を別の語に置き換え、つながりの良い文に直しましょう。(　　) 内に与えられた文字で始まる語を用いた別の表現で言い換えてみましょう。

Nowadays, Japanese *matsuri* attracts not only Japanese people, but also foreign (v　　　　). To truly understand the exciting energy of the (e　　　　), all (t　　　　) have to (d　　　　) is just experience (i　　　　) for themselves.

5. 本文に使われている語で、(　　) 内に与えられた文字で始まる語の挿入で要約文を完成させましょう。ただし、本文の語の品詞を変える必要がある箇所もあります。

In Japan, nearly 300,000 *matsuri* take place 1(a　　　　). They used to be a religious 2(r　　　　), but currently are enjoyed by 3(o　　　　) people as an 4(e　　　　). In a *matsuri, mikoshi* is carried in the town to make an 5(i　　　　) tour for a god. Also, people perform a 6(l　　　　) dance called *bon-odori* to 7(w　　　　) ancestors' spirits that are believed to return during this season. In some famous *matsuri*, a large-scale *mikoshi* or a parade of dancers are seen. They 8(a　　　　) even foreign visitors.

Unit 4

Japanese Corporate Culture

Paragraph の基本構造を理解する

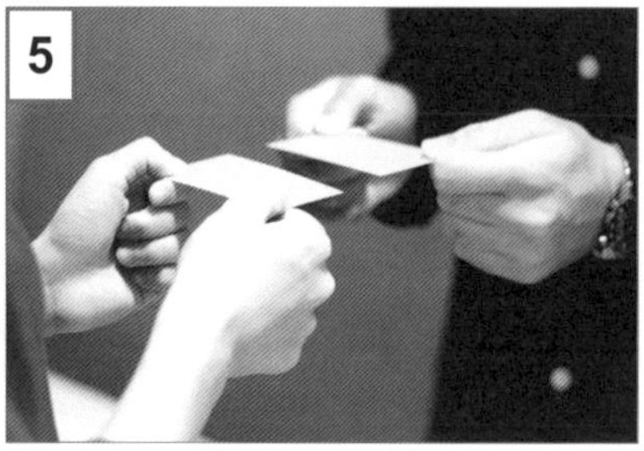

Vocabulary 上の写真を参考に、「企業」に関連しそうな語句を集め、表にまとめてみましょう。似たような意味を持つ語句を複数書いても構いません。

名詞／名詞相当表現	形容詞／形容詞相当表現	動詞／動詞相当表現	副詞／副詞相当表現
· harassment	· economic	· employ	· overtime
· drinking session	· hard-working	· transfer	· loyally
·	·	·	·
·	·	·	·
·	·	·	·
·	·	·	·
·	·	·	·
·	·	·	·
·	·	·	·
·	·	·	·

Pre-Writing

〔　〕内のヒントを参考に、英文を完成させましょう。なお、1～3の（　）には与えられた文字で始まる語が入ります。4～5の［　］では与えられた語句を並べ替えてみましょう。

1) They are all (w　　　　) similar (s　　　　).
〔写真1より：皆同じような服を着ている。〕

2) Their clothes symbolize that they are (n　　　　) (g　　　　) entering the workforce.
〔写真1より：彼らの服は新卒を象徴している。〕

3) They are exchanging their (b　　　　) (c　　　　).
〔写真5より：名刺を交換している。〕

4) Lifetime employment is a system in which [positions / their / until / secure / retirement / employees].
〔終身雇用とは、従業員が退職まで雇用を確保できる制度である。〕

5) The merit system is [employees / to / on / a regime / their achievements / promote / based].
〔実力主義とは、業績に基づく昇進制度である。〕

Drop-by

皆さんは department と聞くと、日本語の「デパート」を思い浮かべるかもしれません。この語は「de」「part」「ment」という3つに分けることができます。「de-」は「分離」のイメージを持つ接頭辞で、「part」は「部分」という意味です。そして「-ment」は名詞を表す接尾辞です。つまり、「部分ごとに分かれたもの」という概念ですので、それに相当する日本語は「部門」「～部」「学科」「～科」「～省」のようになります。日本語の場合は、それぞれ別の語をあてがうのに対し、英語はすべて同じ概念として「department」1つで済ませるわけです。「部門」としてとらえると、「sales department（営業部）」「personnel department（人事部）」など、企業の部署名を表す言葉の一部になりますね（TOEIC ではこの意味でよく出てきます）。「学科」では「psychology department（心理学科）」や「department of business administration（経営学科）」などのように使われます。デパートが「department」ではなく、「department store」になるのは、売り場がそれぞれの部門や小売店ごとに分かれているからです。「部分ごとに分かれたもの」が1つの建物の中に集まったお店、というわけですね。

Grammar 次に示す例文１～２の下線部からわかるように、比較や例示の表現には、書き手の主観的な内容に客観性を持たせる効果が期待できます。

1) This robot is smart. → This robot is as smart as Einstein.
2) There are many foreign students in this university, such as American, German, French, and Chinese students.

次の３～６の各英文に比較や例示の表現を付け加え、客観的な英文にしてみましょう。

3) This microchip is ________ small ________________________.
4) This architectural structure is ________ high ________________________.
5) Eating calorie-rich foods ________________________ makes people fat.
6) This trading policy was adopted by many countries ________________________.

Writing Task 1 次の日本文に合うように、英文中の空欄を埋めてみましょう。なお、(　　) には与えられた文字で始まる語が入ります。

1980 年代、日本経済は好景気を迎えていた。日本企業の特徴的システムである新卒採用、終身雇用、年功序列は、見習うべきモデルとされ、多くの世界的に有名な経済誌で取り上げられた。年功序列とは、従業員が年をとるにつれ自動的に昇進していくシステムであり、これにより「一億総中流」といった現象が生じた。これは国民全員が自分は中流階級のメンバーだと考える現象である。しかし同時に過労死といった深刻な社会問題も出てきた。1990 年代に入り、バブル経済が崩壊すると、以前は称賛されていた日本のシステムは避けるべきモデルとして世界中に認識されるようになった。今、過去と決別するために実力主義を積極的に採り入れる企業も現れている。

In the 1980s, the Japanese economy was prosperous. Japanese companies' unique systems such as new graduate recruitment, lifetime employment, and the seniority system were considered a [1](r　　　　　) [2](m　　　　　) and [3](f　　　　　) in many world-famous economic magazines. The seniority system allows employees to [4](b　　　　　) [5](p　　　　　) automatically as they get older. This collective advancement has caused the phenomenon of *Ichioku-sou-churyu*, which means that all the nation's citizens consider themselves members of the [6](m　　　　　) class. At the same time, however, serious social problems such as *karoshi*, or death from overwork, have appeared. After the [7](b　　　　　) [8](e　　　　　) collapsed in the 1990s, Japan's formerly admired systems became regarded by the international community as mistakes to be avoided. Now, some Japanese companies are actively adopting the [9](m　　　　　) [10](s　　　　　) in order to move on from the past.

Writing Task 2 英語の Essay は「序論」「本論」「結論」という三部構成になっており、本書で想定している 400 語程度の Essay では、最初の Paragraph を序論、最後の Paragraph を結論、残りは本論とするのが一般的です（詳しい構造は Unit 10 で扱います）。本論では、著者の主張をわかりやすく読者へ伝えるために、一般的に次のような構造をとります。

◉ **Topic Sentence:**

その Paragraph で中心となる話題を持ち出し、それについての筆者の意見を述べる

（「その Paragraph で中心となる話題」＝ Topic、「それについての筆者の意見」＝ Controlling Idea）

基本形は「主語（Topic） ＋ be 動詞 ＋ 形容詞（Controlling Idea）」となる

（例：Track-and-field relay races and Japanese *ekiden* are different in several ways.）

（「Track-and-field relay races and Japanese *ekiden*」＝ Topic、「are different in several ways.」＝ Controlling Idea）

◉ **Supporting Sentence(s):**

Topic Sentence で述べた内容の裏付けを短く抽象的にまとめる

（例：For example, the distance that one runner covers is not the same.）

△ **Support(s):**

Topic Sentence の内容の根拠となる具体的なものを提示する（例、数字、データ等）

（例：It is 100 meters in 400 meter track-and-field relay races, while each leg ranges from 8.3 to 22.4 kilometers in the New Year Ekiden.）

◉ **Concluding Sentence:**

その段落で述べてきたことのまとめ、または Topic Sentence の言い換え（ただし本書で扱うような短い Essay では省略されることが多い）

（例：Both sports seem similar but are unique in some respects.）

以下の Paragraph を読み、空欄に入る Topic Sentence を考えてみましょう。

[ ] Some study English because they think the language is necessary to survive in today's globalized society. For example, it brings business opportunities. Others learn English because they want to develop their skill in communicating with foreigners. Improved communication enriches both the personal and professional aspects of their lives. People have multiple motivations to study English.

Writing Task 3 Writing Task 2 の Paragraph の Topic Sentence を支える Supporting Sentence(s)（または Support(s)）が他にないか考え、英文で書いてみましょう。

Japanese Corporate Culture

When the Japanese economy was prosperous, particularly in the 1980s, its corporate culture used to be a role model for other countries which were eager to similarly develop their own economies. It was even featured frequently in world-famous magazines. However, as Japanese economic power declined in the 1990s, this unique culture has instead come to be considered an obstacle to national advancement. This trend has gradually revealed some specific and serious problems with Japanese corporate customs.

Japanese employment practices have been a persistent burden. The traditional hiring model of *shinsotsu-saiyou*, a recruiting limited to new university graduates, has been causing Japanese corporations to lose flexibility in a modern recruiting environment. This system was originally intended to initiate new graduates into their company's principles and nurture their loyalty to their employers. Japanese businesses have tended not to hire workers who had already worked in other organizations and were accustomed to another way of doing things. The lifetime employment system has been another source of trouble. In the 1970s and 80s, employees promised to devote all their time and energy to their corporations, and in return the organizations secured their employment until their retirement. However, this has been preventing talented and ambitious workers from seeking new chances in different businesses and has allowed underproductive employees to stay in the same company.

The promotion process has also been a grave issue. A seniority system allows employees to move up in the organization as they get older regardless of whether they have made significant achievements or not. This practice is supported by collectivism, which is unique to Japanese society and allows every worker to get promoted uniformly. This unique peer mentality has had a negative impact on Japanese companies' management for a long time. Employees worked overtime as a result of pressure from other workers, and the amount of overtime was considered a superficial measurement of their dedication to their institution. Thus, they often prolonged the duration of a task which normally would take only a few hours to complete. This working style, however, is likely to demotivate talented and productive individuals. Instead, particularly after the 2000s, an increasing number of businesses have adopted a merit system; they decide employee promotions on the basis of career backgrounds and achievements instead of age.

As time goes by, the former Japanese corporate culture is gradually becoming obsolete because of its divergence from international standards. The reformation of the Japanese working style has just started.

---

prosperous: 繁栄した　feature:（目玉記事として）取り上げる　specific: 特有の　persistent: 根強い
initiate: 手ほどきする　nurture: 育成する　devote: 捧げる　underproductive: 生産性の低い
grave: 重大な　collectivism: 集団主義　uniformly: 一律に　superficial: 表層的な　dedication: 献身
prolong: 延長する　duration: 継続時間　merit system: 実力主義　adopt: 採用する　obsolete: 陳腐な
divergence: 逸脱

1. "Japanese corporate culture" の言い換えとして用いられている名詞や名詞句を本文中からすべて抜き出しましょう。

2. 下線部に "world-famous magazines" とありますが、これでは具体的なイメージが湧きません。例示の表現を（　　）内に加えてみましょう。

It was even featured frequently in world-famous magazines (　　　　　　　　　　　　　　).

3. 日本の企業文化に対する人々の見方は、1990 年頃を境としてどのように変わったというのでしょうか？下の表を完成させましょう。

1990 年頃より前	経済成長を目指す他の国にとって（　　　　　　　　　　　　　　）。
	上の現象を端的に示す例として（　　　　　　　　　　　　　　）。
1990 年頃より後	（　　　　　　　　　　　　　　）を阻害する。
	（　　　　　　　　　　　　　　）が出てきた。

4. 本文中で述べられていないものは次のうちどれでしょうか。

a. Many Japanese companies did not like to hire employees who had already worked in other companies because these employees tended to stick to their old habits.
b. A lifetime employment system favored the management one-sidedly.
c. Collectivism is one of the essential elements which have constituted the Japanese corporate culture.
d. The old Japanese corporate customs need more examination.

5. この Essay では、伝統的な企業文化がうまく機能しなくなっているため、日本企業が行っている取り組みにはどのようなものがあると述べられているでしょうか。日本語で説明しましょう。

Unit 5

Examination War

Topic Sentence から Supporting Sentences

1

2

3

4

5

6

Vocabulary 上の写真を参考に、「教育」に関連しそうな語句を集め、表にまとめてみましょう。似たような意味を持つ語句を複数書いても構いません。

名詞／名詞相当表現	形容詞／形容詞相当表現	動詞／動詞相当表現	副詞／副詞相当表現
· school rules	· elementary	· prepare	· hard
· cram school	· junior	· follow	· obediently
·	·	·	·
·	·	·	·
·	·	·	·
·	·	·	·
·	·	·	·
·	·	·	·
·	·	·	·
·	·	·	·

Pre-Writing

〔　　〕内のヒントを参考に、英文を完成させましょう。なお、1～3の（　　）には与えられた文字で始まる語が入ります。4～5の［　　］では与えられた語句を並べ替えてみましょう。

1) (T　　　　　) are all wearing school (u　　　　　　).
〔写真1より：皆制服を着ている。〕

2) The (t　　　　　　) from the teacher (d　　　　　　) the students' attention.
〔写真1より：皆先生の話を聴いている。〕

3) The children in yellow school caps are (d　　　　　　) (h　　　　　　) on the street.
〔写真6より：黄色い帽子をかぶった子ども達が道で宿題をしている。〕

4) The Constitution of Japan [to receive / all citizens / education / guarantees / the right].
〔日本国憲法は全国民に教育を受ける権利を保証している。〕

5) A cram school is [students / which / for tests / prepares / an institution].
〔塾とは学生達にテストの準備をさせる施設である。〕

Drop-by

皆さんはpublic schoolと聞くと「（私立ではない）公立校」を思い浮かべるかもしれませんが、イギリスではpublic schoolは上流階級の子どもが入る全寮制の私立のsecondary school（日本の中学校・高等学校に相当）を指します。かつて学校は主に教会に付属し、そこでは僧侶や職人の育成を目的としており、一方貴族の子ども達は主に家庭教師による個人教授を受けていました。近世以降の富裕階級ジェントルマンの勃興により、一般（パブリック）に開かれた学校がつくられていったのがpublic schoolの起源とされています。代表的なものに、Eaton、Harrow、Rugby、Winchester等があり、卒業生の多くはUniversity of Oxford、もしくはUniversity of Cambridgeに進学します。同じsecondary schoolには、公立進学校のgrammar schoolもあります。この名前の由来は、この学校が中世にラテン語の文法（grammar）を教えていた歴史にあるとする説があります。アメリカでは、学費の安さを理由にほとんどの学生がpublic school（「公立校」）に通いますが、裕福な家庭の子どもは、教育の質の高さを求めてprivate school（「私立校」）に入学します。大学も同様の傾向があり、Ivy Leagueに所属する有名大学（Harvard、Yale、Princeton等）は全てprivate universityです。Ivyは植物の「ツタ」という意味ですが、なぜこれらの大学がIvy Leagueと総称されるのでしょうか。インターネットや辞書を使って調べてみましょう。

Grammar

文の内容をより具体的にしたり、同じ語の繰り返しを避けるために、同格・挿入・省略の表現を利用することができます。これにより、2つの文を1つにまとめることができるので、文と文のつながりを整えたり、全体の語数を減らしたりするのに役立ちます。次の各英文を同格・挿入・省略のいずれかの表現を用いて、1つの文にまとめてみましょう。

例）The president had been shot to death. The news shocked all the citizens.

→ The news that the president had been shot to death shocked all the citizens.

1) *Izakaya* is popular with many foreign tourists. It is a Japanese style pub.

→ ……………………………………

2) This school's atmosphere is conservative. However, that school's atmosphere is liberal.

→ ……………………………………

Writing Task 1

次の日本文に合うように、英文中の空欄を埋めてみましょう。なお、(　　) には与えられた文字で始まる語が入ります。

日本の封建時代にあって、国民の社会的、経済的地位は出自によって決定された。しかし、明治維新後、彼らの地位は大学を卒業したかどうか、また彼らの母校の評判に大きく依存するように変化した。第二次世界大戦後、人々は経済的に豊かになり、高等教育を受ける機会が増えたが、それらは日本の中で学歴社会が形成される一因となった。学歴社会とはエリート学校の出身者が優先的に選抜される環境のことを指す。このため親達は、自分の子どもを一流の学校に入れるために必死になって勉強させている。子どもの中には中学校の入学試験を受ける者さえいるが、これに合格するためには「鶴亀算」の知識が必要である。鶴亀算とは、日本の伝統的な計算法で、足の合計の数から鶴と亀それぞれの数を決定する計算法に基づいている。この計算法はたいてい小学校では教えられない。

In the feudal age, Japanese people's social and economic [1](s　　　　) were determined based on their [2](o　　　　). After the Meiji Restoration, however, their [3](s　　　　) began to depend greatly on whether they graduated from universities, and on the prestige of their alma mater. After World War II, people became [4](f　　　　) richer and had more chances to pursue [5](h　　　　) education. This [6](c　　　　) to the formation of an academic [7](m　　　　) in Japan, which means that those who graduate from elite schools are often treated well. It [8](d　　　　) parents to make their children study hard to enter prestigious schools. Some children even take entrance examinations for junior high schools which require knowledge of *tsurukame-zan*, a Japanese [9](t　　　　) method of calculation based on determining the [10](r　　　　) numbers of cranes and tortoises from the total number of their legs. Normally, this [11](c　　　　) method is not even taught in elementary schools.

Writing Task 2

Supporting Sentence は Topic Sentence で示された内容の裏付けを一言で短くまとめたものです。通常はこの後に Support(s) として、根拠を詳しく述べる文が続きます。この Unit では、まず Supporting Sentence のみを取り上げます。

1) To prevent catching the flu, multiple methods are effective. One is to wear a surgical mask in crowds. (Supporting Sentence 1) Another is to gargle after coming back home. (Supporting Sentence 2) Lastly, but most importantly, washing hands frequently is an effective way to prevent transmission of the flu virus. (Supporting Sentence 3)

2) Artificial intelligence (AI) enriches human life for various reasons. First, it potentially reduces the impact of human labor shortages. (Supporting Sentence 1) Next, work performed by AI frees people from the need to work. (Supporting Sentence 2) Last but not least, it does not make mistakes. (Supporting Sentence 3)

以下の 3 つの Topic Sentence から 1 つを選び、その Topic Sentence を裏付ける Supporting Sentence を 3 つ考え、書いてみましょう。

① Too much Internet use is harmful to people's health in some ways.

② Studying abroad brings various positive effects to Japanese young people.

③ A worldwide epidemic negatively impacts the global economy.

Writing Task 3

一般に英語を学習することは重要だと言われています。これを Topic Sentence とし、その考えられる理由 3 つを Supporting Sentence として、それぞれ Topic Sentence と Supporting Sentences を書いてみましょう。

Examination War

Before the end of World War II, the goal of Japanese education was to make loyal citizens, but now fostering patriotic loyalty is not its priority. However, one thing has not changed: the Japanese educational system is a contributing factor to elitism in Japan. Only students who succeed in difficult entrance examinations are allowed to enter schools with an established reputation. This makes Japan a country where entering respected academic institutions is highly competitive.

This competition starts at an early age. Most children enter public elementary schools when six-years-old. [A] At this time, they do not usually need to take any entrance examinations, but at least one percent of the children do take tests for private or national schools. In order to pass those tests, there is a certain kind of preschool or cram school children attend to prepare. [B] For admission at an elite junior high school, the standard elementary school curriculum is not enough. For example, in an arithmetic test, the knowledge of a Japanese traditional method of calculation called *tsurukame-zan* is necessary, but not taught in elementary schools.

The competition only becomes more severe as they get older. [C] Because the number of children has been decreasing rapidly in Japan (it dropped from about two million in 1973 to fewer than one million in 2016), most applicants are able to find a university to offer them acceptance, provided they are not too particular about the institution's standing. However, entering prestigious establishments is still highly competitive; it is common for fewer than one in ten applicants to be accepted and in 2019 some institutions only accepted one in fifty. [D] The competition does not end when they graduate from universities and need to look for a job. New graduates in 2018 interviewed with approximately ten companies and only received an offer from two or three on average.

Japanese entrance examinations are closely related to how this country's educational climate has been formed: educational elitism. Those examinations were originally created to differentiate those who can pass and those who cannot, but their reformation is keenly called for now.

---

patriotic: 愛国的な　contribute: 貢献する　elitism: エリート主義　competitive: 競争的な
admission: 入学　curriculum: 教育課程・カリキュラム　arithmetic: 算数の　standing: 評判
climate:（ある時代・社会の）環境・風潮・傾向　differentiate: 区別する

1. "schools with an established reputation" の言い換えとして用いられている名詞や名詞句を本文中からすべて抜き出しましょう。

2. 下線部はある語が省略されています。その語を補って全体を書いてみましょう。

3. 本文中で述べられていないものは次のうちどれでしょうか。

a. The Japanese educational system creates a group of elites who can study at the most respected academic establishments.
b. Japanese children only need to review what they have learned at school in order to pass prestigious schools' entrance examinations.
c. Japanese high school students can study at a university, if they do not have particular preferences about the university they will enter.
d. Japanese entrance examinations are one of the elements which constitute the present Japanese educational climate.

4. 日本の教育、もしくは入学試験は、日本社会のどういう側面と関わり合ってきたと論じられているでしょうか。日本語で答えましょう。

5. 以下の一文が入る最も適切な場所を、文中の [A] ～ [D] から選びましょう。

After entering junior or senior high schools, most students go to cram schools and prepare for high schools' or universities' entrance examinations.

[　　]

Unit 6

Uniqueness of Japanese Trains

Supporting Sentences から Supports

1

2

3

4

5

6

Vocabulary 上の写真を参考に、「電車」に関連しそうな語句を集め、表にまとめてみましょう。似たような意味を持つ語句を複数書いても構いません。

名詞／名詞相当表現	形容詞／形容詞相当表現	動詞／動詞相当表現	副詞／副詞相当表現
・transportation	・crowded	・come	・on time
・rush hour	・developed	・leave	・punctually
・	・	・	・
・	・	・	・
・	・	・	・
・	・	・	・
・	・	・	・
・	・	・	・
・	・	・	・
・	・	・	・

Pre-Writing

〔　〕内のヒントを参考に、英文を完成させましょう。なお、1～3の（　）には与えられた文字で始まる語が入ります。4～5の［　］では与えられた語句を並べ替えてみましょう。

1) The train is (c　　　　　) with (p　　　　　).
〔写真3より：電車が混んでいる。〕

2) Several people (h　　　　　) on to (h　　　　　) straps.
〔写真3より：多くの人が吊り革につかまっている。〕

3) The (d　　　　　) and the (d　　　　　) time of the train are shown on the electric bulletin board.
〔写真4より：行先と出発時刻が電光掲示板に示されている。〕

4) [major cities / a / the super express / connecting / is / high-speed train].
〔新幹線は主要都市を結ぶ高速鉄道である。〕

5) Passenger load factor is [and / of a vehicle / the actual number / the maximum capacity / the ratio of / of users].
〔乗車率とは、実際の乗客数と定員の割合である。〕

Drop-by

日本の「新幹線」には様々な表記の仕方があります。新幹線を固有名詞と考え、*Shinkansen* と訳すこともあれば、super express（超特急）という語を使うこともあります。一般的には bullet train（弾丸列車）という語が多く用いられているようです。こうした super express や bullet train は列車そのものを指しますが、高速鉄道全体のシステムを指す場合は high-speed rail や rapid transit という表記が用いられます。一方、「高速道路」の英語の表記の仕方は世界中で異なります。例えばアメリカでは、expressway と freeway という2つの表記が一般的なようです。前者は信号機や標識が多少あり、後者はそれらが全くない最上位の高速道路を指します。そのため後者の名前には、使用が無料ということもありますが、「free」（～がない）という語が用いられています。イギリスの高速道路も使用がほとんど無料ですが、motorway という言葉がよく使われています。また、日本語の「路肩」ですが、英語では the shoulder of a road や hard shoulder（主にイギリス）という言葉が使われるそうです。全く同じ表現ですね。

Grammar

英文には「節」と「句」という考え方があります。どちらも２単語以上の意味のまとまりですが、「節」には「主語＋動詞」という要素が含まれ、「句」にはそれが含まれていません。「節」は文が不必要に長くなってしまうことがあるので、その際には「句」に変換すると短くて分かりやすい文になります。例にならって、各英文を「句」の表現に書き換えてみましょう。

例）Because the company introduced a new computer system, its operation goes more smoothly.

→ Thanks to a new computer system, the company's operation goes more smoothly.

例）The rumor that a war breaks out between the two nations made all the citizens nervous.

→ The rumor of a war breaking out between the two nations made all the citizens nervous.

1) A large protest demonstration was held while the journalist was staying in London.

→ ....

2) An athletic meet was canceled because the typhoon was approaching.

→ ....

Writing Task 1

次の日本文に合うように、英文中の空欄を埋めてみましょう。なお、(　　)には与えられた文字で始まる語が入ります。

明治時代以降、日本の交通機関、特に電車は特異な発展を遂げてきた。その特徴の一つは、都市と地方でその発展に大きな差があるということである。都市では公共交通機関は非常に発達しているが、地方では電車が一日に数回しか来ないこともよくある。ただそれが、必ずしも都市に住む人々に快適さを提供しないということもある。朝と夕方のラッシュ時は、電車は非常に混み、乗客達はぎゅうぎゅう詰めになり、息さえもできないことがある。とはいえ、日本の電車は時間に厳格なことでも有名である。電車は時間通り運行するので、時刻表をたよりに家を出れば、目的地に時間通りに着かないことはまずない。こうした特徴により、日本の公共交通機関は、世界でも稀に見る独特なものとなっているのである。

Since the Meiji period, Japanese transportation has been [1](u　　　　　　　) unique development, particularly with regard to trains. One of its characteristics is that there is a huge gap between [2](u　　　　　　　) cities and [3](r　　　　　　　) towns and villages. In the former, public transportation is highly developed, while in the latter, it is often the case that trains come only a few times a day. Even the extensive transportation network in central areas does not necessarily provide [4](c　　　　　　　) to their [5](r　　　　　　　). During the morning and evening rush hours, trains are so crowded that passengers are [6](p　　　　　　　) against each other severely and sometimes even struggle to breathe. However, trains are famous for being [7](p　　　　　　　). They come and go exactly [8](o　　　　　　　) [9](t　　　　　　　). If people leave their home according to the schedule provided, they [10](a　　　　　　　) [11](n　　　　　　　) fail to arrive at their destination in promised time. These aspects make Japanese public conveyance one that is unique globally.

Writing Task 2

このUnitでは、本論中のSupportについて学びます。Support(s)はSupporting Sentence(s)で示された内容の根拠を詳細に述べる部分で、数量、具体例、引用などでSupporting Sentence(s)の妥当性を示します。その際、一貫性を保つために、各文の末尾とそれに続く文の冒頭に関連性があるように書いていきます。また、Supporting Sentenceの冒頭にはTopicとして提示した語句（およびその類語）を用いても構いません。

The location of castles is also a notable characteristic. (Topic Sentence) They were usually constructed on the top of hills in the 15th century. (Supporting Sentence) At that time, the central government's power declined and all of Japan was experiencing territorial disputes between warring states. (Support 1) 「意味的なつながりがある」 To defend against invaders, castles assumed the function of fortress. (Support 2) For that purpose, higher ground proved expedient and these castles came to be called *yama-shiro*, of which Bicchu-Matsuyama-jo is a typical example. (Support 3)

では、以下の①、②のTopic Sentence + Supporting Sentenceから1つを選び、それらに続くSupport(s)を考えて書いてみましょう。

① (Topic Sentence) Japanese society is now an aging society. (Supporting Sentence) This trend is particularly pronounced in rural areas.

② (Topic Sentence) A variety of types of transportation service in Japan have different uses. (Supporting Sentence) Trains, for example, are popular among city residents.

Writing Task 3

Unit 5で考えた、英語を学習することが重要である3つの理由（Supporting Sentences）に、それぞれ1つ（または複数）のSupportを付け加えてみましょう。

Uniqueness of Japanese Trains

In Japan, trains began to run in the Meiji period, when the government's lack of expertise made it initially depend on investment and knowledge from foreign countries. Since then, the Japanese railway industry has developed in its own way. There are some unique points about this transportation network. [A]

First, rural and urban areas are very different in terms of the development of their railway systems. In rural regions the decreasing population, especially the decline in the number of young people, has prevented or reduced investment in transportation. This is true for cities such as Wakkanai in Hokkaido and the state of the JR Souya-Honsen and other local railway lines. Meanwhile, in Tokyo, for example, there are as many as seventy-eight railway lines: sixty-three aboveground lines and fifteen underground lines. This high level of development allows people in urban areas to go anywhere they want by train. [B]

However, this public conveyance does not always provide conveniences to people. In the Tokyo metropolitan area, several million people daily use these highly developed public services to commute to and from their workplaces or schools at the same time. As a result, trains are exceptionally crowded during these times of day. At the morning rush hour peak in 2018, average passenger load factor reached 199% between Kiba and Monzen-nakacho stations in Tokyo, according to a report released by Japanese Ministry of Land, Infrastructure, Transport and Tourism. [C]

Finally, this railway network system is operated precisely on time. The annual average delay time of the Tokaido Shinkansen, a Japanese bullet train, was only about one minute in 2018. An article from 2017 reports that when a Japanese train left a station earlier than the scheduled time by twenty seconds, the operating company apologized officially. This article also describes how overseas people reacted to this incident in Japan. [D]

Japanese trains are unique in some ways: differences in the level of development between rural and urban areas, excessive crowdedness during the rush hours, and the strict punctuality. If you compare the Japanese railway system with that of other countries, you will surely rediscover the former's uniqueness and appreciate its good points.

---

expertise: 専門知識　passenger load factor: 乗車率
Japanese Ministry of Land, Infrastructure, Transport and Tourism: 国土交通省

1. “trains” の言い換えとして用いられている名詞や名詞句を本文中からすべて抜き出しましょう。

2. 第 4 段落の下線部を句に書き換えてみましょう。

This article also describes

3. 以下の一文が入る最も適切な場所を、文中の [A] ～ [D] から選びましょう。

Some were shocked about the way the company dealt with the problem, some exclaimed that its too self-deprecating response was impossible in their own countries, and others commented that it was one of the best things about Japan.

[　　]

4. 本文の内容と一致するものは次のうちどれでしょうか。

a. The developed railway system enriches Japanese people’s life in every respect.
b. The developed train network encourages Japanese people to own private cars.
c. A Japanese train company apologized because its train arrived at a station later than the scheduled time.
d. The punctuality of the Japanese train system is highly appreciated especially when it is compared with that of other countries.

5. この Essay を読んで、日本の電車の特徴的な点、さらにそれぞれの Support に相当する部分を日本語で下の表にまとめてみましょう。

特徴①	
Support	
特徴②	
Support	
特徴③	
Support	

Unit 7

The Key to Long Life

本論の展開方法を覚える１：理由や根拠

1

2

3

4

5

6

Vocabulary 上の写真を参考に、「健康と暮らし」に関連しそうな語句を集めて、表にまとめてみましょう。似たような意味を持つ語句を複数書いても構いません。

名詞／名詞相当表現	形容詞／形容詞相当表現	動詞／動詞相当表現	副詞／副詞相当表現
・building	・busy	・grill	・calmly
・vegetable	・cold	・work	・slowly
・	・	・	・
・	・	・	・
・	・	・	・
・	・	・	・
・	・	・	・
・	・	・	・
・	・	・	・
・	・	・	・

Pre-Writing 〔　　〕内のヒントを参考に、空欄を補うのに最も適切な語句を書きましょう。（　　）には１語、［　　］には複数の語が入り、それぞれ与えられた文字で始まります。

1) Restoring historical architecture means more than accomplishing the (r   ) of the (b   ).
〔写真２より：歴史的建造物の再建には、修復事業の達成以上の意味がある。〕

2) High altitude influences the human body with its lack of (o   ) and cold (c   ).
〔写真３より：標高が高いところは、酸素が薄く、気候も寒いため、人の生活に影響を与える。〕

3) Volunteering gives elderly people the (o   ) to (a   ) interact with others.
〔写真５より：ボランティア活動は高齢者が積極的に人々と関わる良い機会になる。〕

4) An aging-population is a society where the (m   ) of citizens are considerably (o   ).
〔人口の大部分が高齢となっていく社会を高齢化社会という。〕

5) Life expectancy is the estimated [l   ] people are considered [t   ].
〔寿命は人が何歳まで生きるかの予想の元に成り立つ。〕

Drop-by

近年の健康志向や倫理的解釈の変化から食に対する人々の考え方も多様になってきています。その代表的なものが菜食主義ですが、これも実は細かく分けられているのです。完全菜食主義とは野菜類以外は一切摂取しない志向を指し、これを vegan と言います。一般的な菜食主義（vegetarian）は野菜と卵などの乳製品を主食とします。魚菜食主義という区分もあり、文字通り魚肉を食べるこうした人は pescatarian と呼ばれます。基本形を菜食にしつつ時折肉食にもなるという、もはや普通の食生活では ... と思わせる人々は flexitarian を名乗ります。日本食は元来「四つ足の獣の肉」を食べないという風習があったので、魚菜食主義者には順応が楽な食文化かもしれません。しかし、菜食主義のゲストを迎える時などは注意が必要です。というのも、日本食に欠かせない出汁には魚が使われていることも多く、鰹節なども菜食主義の人に振舞ってはいけません。また魚卵も良くお皿を彩っていますが、菜食主義の人々が許容するのは鶏卵なので、これも避けるべき食材です。聞くところによると、鴨（duck）、鶉（quail）、鵞鳥（goose; 複 geese）や駝鳥（ostrich）などの卵も OK のようです。その線引きが「堅い殻があるから」とのことなので、身近にそのような人がいたら真偽を確かめて下さい。

Grammar

次に示す英文を、日本語訳を参考に、指示に従って書き換えてみましょう。

1) The promotion process also deserves attention.

〔昇進制度は注目すべき問題です。従業員たちは年功序列制度によって地位を向上していきます〕

→ ＜ The employees を主語にして下線部を英訳してみましょう＞

....

しかしながら、1 で作成した文では、従業員が主語になってしまうと話題の焦点が曖昧になってしまっています。そこで ...

2) → ＜ A seniority system を主語にして 1 の英文を書き換えてみましょう＞

....

....

Writing Task 1

次の日本文に合うように、英文中の空欄を埋めてみましょう。なお、(　　) には与えられた文字で始まる 1 語、[　　] には指定数の語が入ります。

世界は途上国と先進国に二分されます。前者の生活環境がなかなか改善されない一方で、後者は技術の進歩によって人々の住みやすい社会が実現されています。それを明確に表す証拠として、先進国では長生きが当たり前のようになっています。また、生存率が向上していることと、ひとつの家庭が必ずしも多くの労働力を必要としていないことから、出生率が低下しています。人口全体としての年齢バランスを保つことは、発展国が進歩を続ける上で重要となります。

The world is [1](d　　　　　　) into developing countries and developed countries. Whereas the [2](f　　　　　　) struggles to improve their living environment, the [3](l　　　　　　) keeps cultivating their standard of living to [4](r　　　　　　) a better society. One [5](f　　　　　　) that proves this situation is the longevity of lives for people in developed countries. [6](B　　　　　　) rates are also decreasing in developed countries, caused by an increase in [7](s　　　　　　) rate and low requirements for the [8](w　　　　　　) in each family. [9][3 words:　　　　　　　　　　　　] of the age in population as a whole is crucial for the developed countries to sustain their advancement.

Writing Task 2 無生物主語とは、人や生き物以外が文中の主語となる場合を指します。日本語には稀な表現なので以下のような注意を忘れないようにしましょう。

生物主語：自ら行動**する** ⇅ 無生物主語：他者によって行動**させられる**

無生物を主語に定めるとしても、決して命のない物が勝手に動くのではなく、「他者（もしくはその行動）により影響を受ける」という内容が表現されます。つまり、「A君は知識を得るために勉強をする」が「勉強はA君に知識を与える」のように主体性がなくなるのです。

無生物主語構文で主語になるものは一般名詞の他にも、原因や理由、条件や手段、時や場所などです。これを利用することで、because や if など節の表現を避けることができます。また、文と文のつながりをよくするためにも応用ができます。

次の例を参考に (1) – (3) の書き換えから、日本語で的確に訳すための言葉遣いなども考えてみましょう。

（例） Currently, people can live longer than before.
People are able to live longer because of the advanced society.
→ The advanced society makes it possible for people to live longer.
（和訳：発展した社会によって人々は長生きできる）

(1) The young find it difficult to continue their jobs.
The young are prevented from living comfortably because of stress.
→ Stress ______________________.
（和訳：　　　　　　　　　　）

(2) People in some developing countries are fortunate to have a good water system.
The villagers can acquire clean water if they walk for a few minutes.
→ A few minutes' walk ______________________.
（和訳：　　　　　　　　　　）

(3) The older generation is freed from physically demanding tasks by the sound infrastructure.
→ The sound infrastructure ______________________.
（和訳：　　　　　　　　　　）

Writing Task 3 [　　] 内の語を主語にし、(　　) 内の語句を活用し、以下に続く二つの文を書いてみましょう。

[テレビ] (family members) (main living room)

____

[個室] (individuals) (time)

____

The Key to Long Life

The average life expectancy is extremely high in Japan. The country holds the third place in the world, with men over 80 and women close to 90 years old. One of the reasons for the continual and gradual increase in lifespan is the advancement in medical technologies. If the quality of treatment for illness were closely related to longevity, then well-developed large cities with extensive medical resources, such as Tokyo, Osaka, or Fukuoka, would be expected to emerge as the areas of Japan with the longest living populations. However, this hypothesis is not proved to be true by the statistics. What is hidden behind this phenomenon?

Okinawa was formerly famous as a place with long life expectancies. The warm climate and its residents' humble manner of living, combined with the traditional diet of low fat and highly nutritious food, were the ideal environment in which to foster such a characteristic. Nevertheless, this recognition became a myth after Okinawa was exposed to large quantities of fast food imported from foreign countries. This change of circumstances shows that a good diet is key to avoiding lifestyle-related diseases and subsequently extending life expectancies.

Nagano Prefecture, once ranked low, is now placed high on the national list for this matter. It succeeded in changing the eating habits of its citizens. People in Nagano were prone to heart disease because of the custom of high salt consumption, which is typical in cold and mountainous areas in Japan. Additionally, inhabitants could not easily engage in mentally stimulating active pastimes due to reduced mobility in the aging-population and heavy winter snowfall. Nagano Prefecture residents needed to be satisfied not only with their diets but psychologically as well. To change this downward spiral, the locals of the area first reduced the amount of their salt intake. Then, for their mental satisfaction, municipal councils arranged for volunteer work for the older population so that they remain mentally stimulated.

The combination of both physical and mental health is the secret to long life. Nonetheless, urban areas that tend to focus more on the young than the old fail to accept this notion. It is for this reason that the major cities in Japan cannot be ranked high in terms of life expectancy, despite having high standards of medical treatment. Should more people be concerned with their diets? Should you abandon fatty or salty foods, even if they are satisfying? What do you think about the relationship between long life and quality of life?

---

lifespan: 寿命　longevity: 長寿　emerge: 現れる　hypothesis: 仮説　phenomenon: 現象
nutritious: 栄養価が高い　ideal: 理想の　foster: 育む　expose: 晒す　subsequently: 結果として
extend: 延長する　consumption: 消費　mountainous: 山間の　spiral: 螺旋　intake: 摂取
stimulate: 活気づける　abandon: 諦める

1. ‘life’ に関係する語句を本文中から全て抜き出しましょう。

2. 下線部を無生物主語により英語として自然な流れになるよう書き換えましょう。“prevent” の語形を変えたものが追加されると良いです。

inhabitants could not easily engage in mentally stimulating active pastimes due to reduced mobility in the aging-population and heavy winter snowfall.

3. 第 1 段落の this hypothesis が示すものとして正しいものを以下から選びましょう。

a. A large percentage of the population secures long lives.
b. Medical technology is not the only factor for extending people’s lives.
c. Developed cities can make people’s lives longer.
d. Pollution in urban areas is shortening the lives of people.

4. 第 2 段落の this recognition が示すものとして正しいものを以下から選びましょう。

a. People in Okinawa are living quiet and simple lives.
b. The main diet for the people in Okinawa is fast food.
c. People in Okinawa have largely moved to bigger cities in Japan.
d. The life expectancy in Okinawa is remarkable.

5. 第 1 段落最後の What is hidden behind this phenomenon? に答えるため、以下の空欄を埋めてみましょう。

The key to long life is not only the advancement of the [1]( ) ( ).

The important aspects for realizing this goal are to maintain a [2]( ) ( ) and keep a stable [3]( ) ( ).

辞書の使い方（2）

山田　茂

電子辞書の例文検索

携帯型の電子辞書の「例文検索」機能を使えば、文法や品詞がわからなくても意味を探すことができる。特に、成句やコロケーションの検索に有効である。例えば手許の電子辞書（XD-K18000）で左の検索語を入力すると、右の結果がヒットする：

「trade&talk*」→「trade talks 通商会談」（『新編英和活用大辞典』）
「talk&progress*」→「The summit talks collapses [progressed]. 首脳会談は失敗に終わった［進展した］」（『ジーニアス大英和辞典』）

これらを活用すると最初の例文の意味が以下のように導き出せる：

Trade <u>talks</u> are progressing well. 通商会談は順調に進んでいる。

*「例文検索」の成功率を高めるため、名詞は単数形、動詞・形容詞は原形を入力する。また、冠詞、代名詞など周辺的で変わりうる要素は入力しない。

発信（作文）のための辞書の使い方

英語での発信を行う際、コロケーションがキーとなる。コロケーションとは、語と語の相性の意味で、近年英語辞書でも広く扱われている。例えば、「列車は速度を増した」と言いたいのだが、適切な動詞がわからないとしよう。どの辞書で何を引けばいいか？

The train (　　　　　) speed.

以下のような二つのアプローチが可能だ：

● 同義語で引く
- 和英辞典で「増す」を引く。
- 類義語辞典（例:*Longman Language Activator*）で、「増す」に当たる語（例:increase）を引いてみる。

● コロケーションで引く
- コロケーション辞典で speed を引き、一緒に使われる動詞を検索する。
- 英和辞典、学習英英辞典で speed を引き、例文の中から適切な動詞を探す。

コロケーション辞典

コロケーションに特化した辞書がある。『新編英和活用大辞典』、外国人学習者向けの *Oxford Collocations Dictionary for Students of English* は大学生向けの電子辞書には入っているだろう。

コロケーションは下記の通り「連結語＋基語」の組み合わせであるが、コロケーション辞典を使う際は基語で引く。「名詞があれば名詞で引く」と覚えておくとよい：

	基語	>	連結語	
形＋名：	**名**	>	形	strong **coffee**
動＋名：	**名**	>	動	consult a **dictionary**
前＋名：	**名**	>	前	in a **handout**
動＋副：	**動**	>	副	**drink** heavily
副＋形：	**形**	>	副	deeply **grateful**

それでは先程の問題に取り組んでみよう。Oxford のコロケーション辞典で speed を引き、相性のよい動詞を探してみよう。以下のような情報が得られ、2 番目のグループの動詞（build up, gain, gather, increase, pick up）が該当することがわかる。

VERB + SPEED

attain, reach
- *The car reaches a speed of 60 miles per hour within five seconds.*

| build up, gain, gather, increase, pick up
- *The train pulled out of the station, slowly gathering speed.*

| lose | curb, kill, reduce
- *measures to curb the speed of cars travelling through the village*

| maintain
- *The boat maintained a steady speed while the sea was calm.*

| measure
-

Oxford Collocations Dictionary for Students of English の speed の項目

上級者には、無料でアクセスできる Skell (Sketch Engine for Language Learning, https://skell.sketchengine.co.uk/run.cgi/skell) の Word Sketch もお勧めする。

電子辞書：「日本語のキーワードで英語の例文を探す」

この機能は英和・和英辞典に収録されている英語の例文を日本語ベースで検索するというすぐれものだ。先程の問題を解くために、手許の電子辞書で「速度」と「増す」を入力してみると、以下のような例文がヒットした：

pick up [gather] speed（次第に）速度を増す（『ウィズダム英和辞典』）

列車は速度を増した The train gained [gathered] speed.（『ジーニアス和英辞典』）

おわりに

英英辞典で語句を引き直してみると、思わぬ発見をすることがある。現在、代表的な学習英英辞典（Cambridge, Collins, Longman, Macmillan, Merriam-Webster, Oxford）がウェブ上に無料で公開されている。また、携帯型電子辞書には英英辞典、類義語辞典、コロケーション辞典が搭載されており、ジャンプ機能を使えば、わからない英単語を英和辞典でチェックできる。例文検索他の有用な機能も備わっている。「検索」を「学び」のチャンスととらえ、質・幅共に辞書検索の技術を高め、英語力の向上に役立ててほしい。

参考文献

Hartmann, R. R. K. 2001. *Teaching and Researching Lexicography*. Pearson Education.

山田茂．2014．『学習英英辞典活用の手引き：英語教育における効果的な辞書指導のヒント』オックスフォード大学出版局.

山田茂．2020．『OALD10 活用ガイド：辞書編』旺文社.

Unit 8

Distinct Style or Neglect of Identity

本論の展開方法を覚える２：時系列

1

2

3

4

5

6

Vocabulary 上の写真を参考に、「ファッションや流行」に関連しそうな語句を集めて、表にまとめてみましょう。似たような意味を持つ語句を複数書いても構いません。

名詞／名詞相当表現	形容詞／形容詞相当表現	動詞／動詞相当表現	副詞／副詞相当表現
· clothes	· beautiful	· spread	· happily
· birds	· colorful	· laugh	· lively
·	·	·	·
·	·	·	·
·	·	·	·
·	·	·	·
·	·	·	·
·	·	·	·
·	·	·	·
·	·	·	·

Pre-Writing

〔　　〕内のヒントを参考に、空欄を補うのに最も適切な語句を書きましょう。（　　）には１語、［　　］には複数の語が入り、それぞれ与えられた文字で始まります。

1) European style dress became a part of Japanese culture after the (e　　　　　　) of the Meiji (e　　　　　　).
〔写真１より：西洋のドレスは明治政府の誕生後に日本文化の一部となった。〕

2) To enchant others means showing an (a　　　　　) feature to capture their (a　　　　　).
〔写真２より：他者を魅了するということは、魅力でもって好感を得ることである。〕

3) Group work requires an equal (s　　　　　) of effort and (r　　　　　).
〔写真５より：グループワークでは努力と責任が等分されているべきである。〕

4) Sustained isolation was the time when Japan closed its (d　　　　　) to the (o　　　　　) world.
〔鎖国とは日本が海外に対して外交の扉を閉ざしていた時期である。〕

5) Westernization is a movement in which the [c　　　　　　　　　] of the West impact [a　　　　　　　　　].
〔西洋化は渡来の文化や趣向がある地域に影響を及ぼす動きのことである。〕

Drop-by

洋服の文化が日本に勢い良く流入してきた時期は開国時ですが、それに伴い日本語の中にこれまで存在していなかった様々な用語が盛り込まれるようになりました。しかし、単語の語源を理解し、和製英語かどうかの判断をしなければ、カタカナ語が英語圏の人々に伝わらないことや別の意味で捉えられてしまうこともあります。Unit 9 の本欄でも紹介するズボンは元々フランス語の jupon から来ており、これは女性がスカートの下に履くペチコートのことです。トレーナーと聞くと、日本ではスウェット地で出来た長袖ですが、英語では sweatshirt と言い、生地の名称が明示されます。trainers はイギリス英語で運動靴のことです。同様の靴がアメリカ英語では sneakers になるので、日本語のスニーカーとは同じですね。頭を覆う布の付いたパーカーなどはイヌイット語が語源で、英語では hoodie が正解です。女性のワンピースも、元々は one-piece dress として日本に入ってきたものから dress が省略されたのですが、英語圏で削っていいのは one-piece の方で、総じて dress と呼ばれます。上の運動靴の例に見られるように、名称は英米での違いもあり、セーターが sweater とアメリカで言われるのに対し、イギリスでは jumper となります。日本語のジャンパーは windbreaker や jacket を指します。これをきっかけにカタカナ語を見直してみるのも面白いかもしれません。

Grammar 次に示す英文を、説明文を参考に＜　＞内の指示に従って書き換えてみましょう。

Most castles in Japan are built on solid stone foundations.
〔日本の城の多くは頑丈な石垣の上に建てられている。〕

1) 多くの地震に見舞われるので、柔らかい建築材が求められる。

→ ＜上の英文に続くような一文を書きましょう（与えられた語は必要に応じて形を変えること）＞
material / have / flexible / wood / require / earthquake / frequent

.... to be used for the construction.

2) その技術によって城は長きにわたって支えられている。

→ ＜1の英文に続くような一文を書きましょう（与えられた語は必要に応じて形を変えること）＞
long / the / castle / technique / enable / remain / to / the

....

Writing Task 1 次の日本文に合うように、英文中の空欄を埋めてみましょう。なお、(　　) には与えられた文字で始まる1語、[　　] には指定数の語が入ります。

1853年にマシュー・C・ペリーが浦賀港に来航するまで、200年以上もの間、日本は鎖国していた。とはいえ完全な閉鎖ではなかったため、他国と部分的に微かな文化の融合をしながら、独自の文化を作り上げていった。服装でいえば、明治時代に至るまでは着物と草履が活用されていた。男性の髪型である髷が江戸の終わりとともに失われた一方で、女性の日本髪は形、職業、機会などを変えながら、今日でも生き続けている。今となってはそれも海外からの観光客を惹きつける魅力的な日本文化の一つとなっている。

Until 1853 when Matthew C. Perry arrived in Uraga Bay, the country of Japan isolated [1](i　　　　　) from the world for more than 200 years. Since it was not a complete [2](c　　　　　), the island developed its unique culture, [3](p　　　　　) and [4](s　　　　　) mixing various external cultural elements. In [5](t　　　　　) of outfits, before reaching the Meiji era, Japanese people essentially wore *kimono* and sandals. Although the *mage* topknot hairstyle for males [6](d　　　　　) out with the end of Edo era, the *nihon gami* hairstyle for females [7](s　　　　　) to continue even today by adjustments to its styling, as well as the [8](p　　　　　) and occasions where it is featured. Now, it has become [9][4 words　　　　　　　　　　　　　　　　] that is attractive to foreign visitors.

Writing Task 2

分詞構文は、原則として「分詞から始まる句」と主語・動詞を含む「主節」の組み合わせで使われます。「タイミング」や「原因」を表現する際に使われることが多いです。

タイミング

出来事Aが起こった時 → 出来事Bが起こる = Opening the country, Japan adopted Western culture.
（開国した時、西洋文化が流入した）

原因

原因Aがあったため → 結果Bが起こる = Having little influence from abroad, Japanese culture became unique.
（海外からの影響が最小限だったため、日本文化は独特なものとなった）

分詞構文が表す意味は時・理由・条件など幾つかありますが、それらは結局ものごとの因果関係を表現することになります。接続詞に導かれる従属節が不要になるため、文意を変えずに表現が短くできます。これで単文（「主語＋述部」が１つ）を幾つも繋げていくのではなく、複文（「主語＋述部」が複数）にまとめることが可能なのです。また、句の部分を主語の後に挿入することもあるので、これを使って、文の流れを整えることができます。

次の (1) – (3) の英文作成から接続詞を加えるパターンや、否定のパターンも身につけましょう。

(1) There are various fashion companies around the world.
The products of major brands are expensive, because they are imported from abroad.
［分詞構文を用いて書き換え］
→ (expensive / being / from / are / major / imported / brands / fashion / abroad)

（和訳：　　　　　　　　　　）

(2) The innovative style occasionally creates a new trend.
New styles are popular among the young.
However, the older people do not welcome new styles.
［上の文に続く二文を一文にまとめることで、new styles の重複を防ぐ］
→ (popular / generations / the / while / among / being / young)

→ (older / styles / are / people / by / unwelcomed / new)

（和訳：　　　　　　　　　　）

(3) A professor and a student met in the university campus.
Then, they agreed to start a unique project. ［分詞構文 (meeting) を使って二文を一文に］

（和訳：　　　　　　　　　　）

Writing Task 3

キーワードをヒントに、因果関係が含まれる文を書いてみましょう。

［家族］→

［収入］→

Distinct Style or Neglect of Identity

The first purpose of Clothes [...] was not for warmth or decency, but for ornament. (Thomas Carlyle. *Sartor Resartus: The Life and Opinions of Herr Teufelsdröckh.* Chapter V. The World in Clothes. 1836)

As Thomas Carlyle once wrote, fashion is crucial to people because it allows them to use an array of fabrics to make themselves [(1)]. In this respect, fashion functions similarly to the bright feathers of peacocks. Males fan out their tail-feathers to attract females during the mating season. Regardless of gender, animals seem to be less eager to impress others than humans. People have constantly involved themselves in developing unique features of their appearances, sometimes resulting in the creation of collective fashion styles.

Japan has a special history in this field. The Japanese people focused on their own clothing culture like the *kimono* since the country was forced into a sustained isolation for more than 200 years until 1853. However, the end of seclusion meant the beginning of modernization, in other words, the arrival of [Westernization]. After almost entirely abandoning traditional Japanese clothing except for special professions and ceremonial occasions, the trend was to imitate the current Western fashion. Starting with samurais cutting off their pony-tail hairstyle and changing their sandals to boots, Western clothing became dominant in just half a century, miniskirts were fashionable in the 1960s, hippie styles arrived in the 1970s, and body-conscious fashions became prominent in the 1980s and the 90s.

From the mid-1990s, Japanese teenagers' taste started to greatly dominate the trends. Hundreds of students in uniquely decorated school uniforms gathered in urban centers like Shibuya in Tokyo. Girls with loose socks in particular were seen wearing high-brand cardigans and scarves. They eventually embraced an appearance featuring extremely tanned skin with wide white eyeliner and lipstick, a style known by the name *yamanba-gyaru* (monstrous gals).

There is another trend which accurately represents the personality of modern Japanese. This is named *ryosan-gata* (a depersonalized mass-produced fashion). This does not mean wearing mass-produced clothing, such as fast fashion. Instead, this term refers to many consumers from the same age group choosing almost identical outfits. Due to a strong attachment to their uniforms, these people have a tendency to feel insecure about looking differently from the rest of their peers. Thus, the young follow the trend for uniformity established during their teenage years. Some post-high school students maintain a similar external appearance even when out of uniform in order to blend in with others. This similarity is not limited to their clothing, but also extends to hairstyles, make-up, and how they wear accessories.

Japan is in the interesting situation of having featureless fashion as the defining feature of a generation.

---

decency: 上品さ　ornament: 飾り　array: 衣装　abandon(ing): 遺棄する　profession(s): 職業
ceremonial: 儀式の　imitate: 模倣する　prominent: 傑出した　dominate: 支配する
eventually: 最終的に　embrace(d): 受け入れる　attachment: 愛着　peer(s): 同輩　external: 外側の

1. 'fashion' に関係する語句を本文中から全て抜き出しましょう。

2. 波線部を分詞構文で英語として自然な流れになるよう書き換えましょう。

the young follow the trend for uniformity established during their teenage years. Some

3. 第１段落の （1） に当てはまるものとして正しいものを以下から選びましょう。

a. blend in with others
b. disappear as an individual
c. stand out from the rest
d. become less vulnerable to weather

4. 第２段落の Westernization によって起こったことの中で正しいものを以下から選びましょう。

a. The Japanese culture was overwritten entirely.
b. The Western tradition was isolated from Japan
c. The people from abroad started to dominate one area of Japan.
d. The culture of the West was combined with Japanese culture.

5. 冒頭にある not for warmth or decency, but for ornament の説明として、以下の空欄を埋めてみましょう。

The reason for people to wear certain [1]( ) is not for its [2]( ) and [3]( ), but to [4]( ) his or her distinctiveness to [5]( ) the attention of [6]( ).

Unit 9

Drinking Rituals

本論の展開方法を覚える３：意見の並列

1

2

3

4

5

6

Vocabulary 上の写真を参考に、「お酒」に関連しそうな語句を集めて、表にまとめてみましょう。似たような意味を持つ語句を複数書いても構いません。

名詞／名詞相当表現	形容詞／形容詞相当表現	動詞／動詞相当表現	副詞／副詞相当表現
・rice	・calm	・pour	・quietly
・cup	・crowded	・walk	・excessively
・	・	・	・
・	・	・	・
・	・	・	・
・	・	・	・
・	・	・	・
・	・	・	・
・	・	・	・
・	・	・	・

Pre-Writing

〔　　〕内のヒントを参考に、空欄を補うのに最も適切な語句を書きましょう。(　　) には１語、[　　] には複数の語が入り、それぞれ与えられた文字で始まります。

1) The barrels of alcohol are (o　　　　　) lined in Japanese (s　　　　　) and (t　　　　　).
〔写真１より：日本の神社や寺では整然と並べられた酒樽が見られる。〕

2) When (t　　　　　) in Japan, people with junior status (h　　　　　) their cup with (b　　　　　) hands.
〔写真３より：乾杯するとき日本では部下や後輩は両手で杯を持つべきとされる。〕

3) Fully (b　　　　　) cherry blossoms in the park are (i　　　　　) with (d　　　　　) lights.
〔写真４より：公園の満開の桜はイルミネーションライトで彩られている。〕

4) The head of the table is the seat where the most (i　　　　　) (g　　　　　) is placed.
〔上座には重鎮が座する。〕

5) Middle ground is a place where multiple people [a　　　　　　　　　　].
〔中庸とは人々が妥協を受け入れられるポイントである。〕

Drop-by

日本では「読書の秋」「スポーツの秋」「食欲の秋」「芸術の秋」などと言われますが、この認識は日本の通説で、必ずしも海外でそのまま通じるとは限りません。秋は日が暮れるのが早くなり、夜が長くなることから読書に適していることは万国共通かもしれません。しかし、「スポーツ」は 1964 年の東京オリンピック以来 10 月 10 日が体育の日に定められたこと、「食欲」は日本食に適した食材の収穫が秋ということが原因となっています。「芸術」は絵画の展示会が多く秋に設けられていた古い習慣が関係しています。独自の表現といえば、全員ではないにしろアメリカ英語は秋を fall で言い表し、イギリス英語では autumn を使います。同じ英語でも二国間で意味が変わってくるものもあるので、幾つか知っておくと良いでしょう。例えば、道端などで見かけるゴミ箱をアメリカで trash (can) と言うのに対し、イギリスではこれを bin と呼び、乾いたゴミを rubbish、生ゴミは garbage と言い、アメリカで言う trash はあまり聞かないかもしれません。他にも You should use the turn signal now because there is a spot in the parking lot.（そこに駐車スペースがあるんだから、指示機をいま出さないと）とアメリカ人が言う状況も、イギリスでは You should use the indicator now because there is a space in the car park. となるでしょう。あるいは日本語のズボン（パンツ）はアメリカでは日本でも使われる pants ですが、イギリスでは trousers と言い、pants は下着を指すなど、状況によっては恥ずかしい思いをしてしまうかもしれません。大概は笑い話で済みますが。

Grammar

次に示す英文 a-c を、日本語訳を参考に、＜　＞内の指示に従って書き換えてみましょう。

a) The competition becomes more severe as students get older. b) In addition, tuition fees increase in university. c) Therefore, the burden increases for both children and parents.

1) ＜ In addition を削除して、a) と b) を接続詞でつないでみる＞
競争は学生の年齢が上がるにつれて熾烈になってくる一方で、学費も上がる。

2) ＜ 1 で作成した英文に続けて、c) を分詞構文でつないでみる＞
競争は学生の年齢が上がるにつれて熾烈になってくる一方で、大学の学費も上がり、結果として子供と親の両方が負担を感じることになる。

Writing Task 1

次の日本文に合うように、英文中の空欄を埋めてみましょう。なお、(　　)には与えられた文字で始まる１語、[　　] には指定数の語が入ります。

古くからお酒を飲むような宴の場面は参加者が親睦を深める機会として重宝されてきました。無礼講という言葉はあるものの、羽目を外さないことで人々の品格が示されることもありました。そうした流れの中で飲み会において推奨される振る舞いが決められたとすることもあります。こうした思慮深く考えることこそ日本的と言えるでしょう。そうすれば、日本人としての特色を維持する上でも、宴会のルールも重要性を帯びてくるのです。

[1](F　　　　　　) that include alcoholic drinks are highly valued as an opportunity for the guests to get [2](a　　　　　　) with each other. Although there is a concept of [3][3 words　　　　　　　　　　　　] at certain occasions, people express their [4](d　　　　　　) by not letting themselves go. Thus, various [5](r　　　　　　) for drinking behavior have been [6](e　　　　　　). This considerate [7](t　　　　　　) is one of the typical features of the Japanese people. Then, to [8](p　　　　　　) one's character as a Japanese, manners [9](a　　　　　　) to drinking become significant.

Writing Task 2

接続詞とは、文と文をつなぐ役割を持つ表現です。しかし、使い方を誤ると単調なリズムの連続となってしまいます。効果的な使い方や、無生物主語構文や分詞構文を用いて接続詞を使わずに済ませる方法を考えましょう。

> A) Young people avoid this kind of party because it requires formality.
>
> ⇅
>
> B) Young people avoid this kind of party. Because it requires formality.

話し言葉と書き言葉の認識が混ざってしまっていることから、Bのような「文章」をよく目にします。Because だけではなく、And / But / So なども文頭に置くことは推奨されません。A のように節と節をつなぐような接続詞の使い方を目指し、節の意識を持ちましょう。

ただし、接続詞を伴う文は、無生物主語や分詞構文を使った文よりも長くなりがちです。長い文章は目立つので、論拠として重要な部分や著者の主張など、読者に注意深く読んでもらいたい部分に限るべきです。それ以外は、基本的には無生物主語構文や分詞構文を用いて書くように心掛けましょう。

次の (1) – (4) の日本語を英語で書き換えてみましょう。また和文下のキーワードも参考に英文を考えてみてください。

(1) 20 歳になる前に飲酒することは法で禁じられているので、若者はその時を待ち遠しく思う。

Being banned by law to drink before 20 years of age, teenagers (l   ) (f   ) that moment when they are legally allowed to drink.

(2) アルコールの影響は過度に消費しなければ比較的良いものだ。

The (e   ) of alcohol is relatively (p   ), (u   ) it is consumed (e   ).

(3) 大学生たちは飲む機会に囲まれているが、20 歳になるまでは決して飲んではいけない。

(surrounded by / underage) → ....

(4) 若いゲストは目上の人がパーティーで席に近づいてきた時には立って挨拶すべきだ。

(greet / approach) → ....

Writing Task 3

「お酒」にまつわるイメージを理由とともに法助動詞を使わずに、それでいて自然な接続詞を組み込みながら四文書いてみましょう。

Drinking Rituals

Nowadays, people in Japan can consume a variety of types of alcoholic beverages such as beer, wine, and spirits brought in from abroad. *Sake*, Japanese rice wine, has been available for centuries and now has gained a global reputation. However, Japanese drinking customs are not well-known to the general, non-Japanese public.

The link between Japanese seasons and drinking habits is one notable feature. In the spring, people gather for *hanami*, which are like picnics under beautiful cherry blossoms with *sake*. *Ama-zake* is believed to be good for resisting the scorching heat of the summer. At the end of the hot season, the arrival of the autumn is celebrated with *sake* and ball-shaped rice cakes at *tsukimi*, where people observe the special moon, *chushu-no-meigetsu* (mid-autumn full-moon). In the winter, *yukimi*, drinking while watching the snow, is enjoyed, and the New Year is marked with the performance of *kagami-wari*, which involves breaking open a barrel of *sake*.

Alcohol is also present in religious ceremonies. *Omiki* is an important part of Shinto, an indigenous Japanese religion. Worshipers are believed to receive some strength from the spirits by consuming *omiki*. This drink was initially called *miki*（御酒）, which was a combination of "*mi*"（御）, a prefix that denotes courtesy, and "*ki*," an alternate pronunciation of the character for *sake*（酒）. Later, the prefix for respect "*o*" was added and the character for god（神）replaced "*mi*" as a homophone. These changes created the present *omiki*（御神酒）, which literally means "god's drink".

Alongside seasonal and ceremonial events, the basic accompanying concepts behind drinking have not greatly changed. It is still a sort of ritual and, therefore, there are various rules for younger members. They are indirectly but customarily required (1) to yield the seat at the *kamiza*, the head of the table, to the most senior, superior, influential, or authoritative member; (2) to place the orders and serve them to the group; and (3) to drink whatever they are offered. Most of these rules are now seen as archaic, but they still partially exist in Japanese society. Younger people often express their hesitation to attend functions where drinking is involved because of these seemingly trivial "manners".

If the experience of drinking alcohol comes with a set of manners, which are connected to traditional Japanese rituals, should we strive to preserve these by finding a middle ground between traditional and more current customs, or should we dismiss them altogether as old-fashioned nonsense?

---

beverage: 飲料　scorching: 焼け付くような　barrel: 樽　indigenous: 固有の　worshiper: 信仰者
courtesy: 丁寧　homophone: 異形同音異義語　superior: 上位の　archaic: 古風な　hesitation: 躊躇
dismiss: 退ける

1. ‘event’ に関係する語句を本文中から全て抜き出しましょう。

2. 波線部からbecauseを除いた一文を作ってみましょう。なお[　　]の書き出しで始めてください。

Younger people often express their hesitation to attend functions where drinking is involved because of these seemingly trivial “manners”.
[These trivial “manners” cause younger people to...]

3. 第４段落の seasonal and ceremonial events が示さないものを以下から選びましょう。

a. People gather under cherry trees in full bloom.
b. Worshipers cherish the drink served at the shrine.
c. Both young and old enjoy socializing after a long day’s work.
d. The arrival of winter is marked with the falling snow and a cup of sake.

4. 下記のイディオムの［　　］内の単語を別の単語に変えて似た意味になるようにしましょう。

例）[head] of the table → [top] of the table

a. [place] the orders → [g　　　　　　] the orders
b. [set] of manners → a [r　　　　　　] of manners
c. middle [ground] → middle [z　　　　　　]

5. 第４段落の them が示すものの説明として、以下の空欄を埋めてみましょう。

The [1](　　　　　) guests should distribute [2](　　　　　) to the [3](　　　　　) of each person. They should also [4](　　　　　) (　　　　　) individually according to specific [5](　　　　　).

Unit 10

Traditional Crafts in Japan

序論・本論・結論の役割

1

2

3

4

5

6
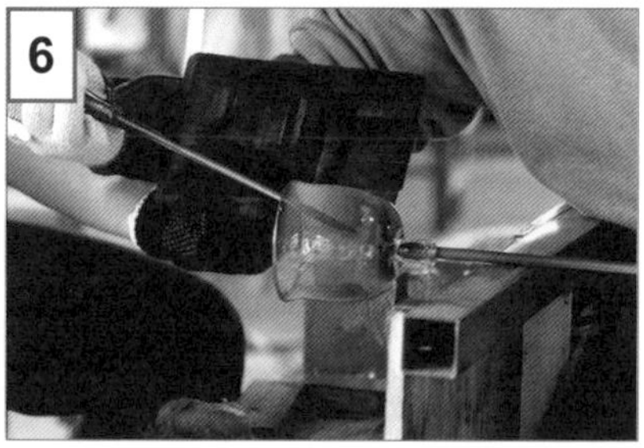

Vocabulary 上の写真を参考に、「伝統工芸品」に関連しそうな語句を集め、表にまとめてみましょう。

名詞／名詞相当表現	形容詞／形容詞相当表現	動詞／動詞相当表現	副詞／副詞相当表現
· tableware	· beautiful	· make	· exquisitely
· paper lantern	· traditional	· display	· traditionally
·	·	·	·
·	·	·	·
·	·	·	·
·	·	·	·
·	·	·	·
·	·	·	·
·	·	·	·
·	·	·	·

Pre-Writing 〔　　〕内のヒントを参考に、空欄を補うのに最も適切な語句を書きましょう。（　　）には1語、［　　］には複数の語が入り、それぞれ与えられた文字で始まります。

1) Japanese lacquerware made by a (m　　　　　) called *Wajima-nuri* is tough enough to (w　　　　　) centuries of use.
〔写真2より：「輪島塗」という技法で作られた漆器は数百年に及ぶ使用にも耐えられるほど丈夫だ。〕

2) *Noren* at the entrance of a shop (i　　　　　) that it is open for (b　　　　　).
〔写真3より：店先に暖簾が出ているのでその店は営業中だ。〕

3) Glassware is (s　　　　　) at an extremely high (t　　　　　).
〔写真6より：ガラス製品は非常に高温の状態で成形される。〕

4) A woodcrafter is an artisan who (p　　　　　) wood into tableware and (f　　　　　).
〔木工職人とは木材を加工して食器や家具を作り出す職人のことだ。〕

5) *Kokeshi* colors and shapes vary from [r　　　　　　　　　　], which led to the product also becoming popular as a collectible.
〔こけしは地方によって色彩や造形が異なるため、やがて収集して楽しまれるようになった。〕

Drop-by

自在鳥　明珍宗春　江戸時代　鉄　長 41.0cm

本 Unit の Essay では、日本の伝統工芸品の一つとして「自在置物」が紹介されています。江戸時代には、その多くが明珍派の甲冑師によって製作されていました。現在では満《みつ》田《た》晴《はる》穂《お》や大《おお》竹《たけ》亮《りょう》峯《ほう》といった作家が新作を発表しています。前者は従来通り金属を加工していますが、後者は木材を素材とするなど、両者とも自在置物を単なる伝統工芸品ではなく、超絶技巧を伴う現代アートとして世界に向けてその魅力を発信し続けています。また、キャラクターフィギュアのメーカーとしても知られる「海洋堂」が、龍や不動明王などの自在置物を一般向けに販売しています。

Grammar

次に示す英文を、日本語訳を参考に、〈　　〉内の指示に従って書き換えてみましょう。

1) Most armorers had to change professions because Japan had an extended time without war.
(日本では戦争がなかった時代が長く続いたために、甲冑職人のほとんどが転職せざるを得なかった。)

→ ＜次の語句を主語として＞

Japan's extended time without war ....

2) Therefore, some of them used their metalworking skills to create *jizai okimono.*
(したがって、そのなかには持ち前の金属加工技術を用いて自在置物を作り出した者もいた。)

→ ＜分詞構文を用いて、1 で作成した英文に続け、まとめて 1 つの英文となるように＞

....

Writing Task 1

次の日本文に合うように、空欄を補うのに最も適切な語句を書きましょう。(　　) には 1 語、[　　] には複数の語が入り、それぞれ与えられた文字で始まります。

伊万里焼は、日本の伝統的な磁器有田焼の一種である。佐賀県有田地方で生産されており、伊万里港を経て販売されたためにこの名が付いている。伊万里焼は 1643 年に酒井田柿右衛門が赤絵を確立したことで発達した。17 世紀に造られた古伊万里は国内外で珍重されている。赤絵の上に金彩色を施した「金襴手様式」の古伊万里は主にヨーロッパの貴族に買い求められて、宮殿内の装飾に使われた。柿右衛門様式の伊万里焼はヨーロッパの焼き物にも影響を及ぼし、ドイツのマイセン窯、オランダのデルフト窯など各国でその様式が取り入れられた。

Imari is a kind of traditional Japanese porcelain known as Arita [1](w　　　　　). These ceramics, produced in the Arita [2](r　　　　　) of Saga, passed through Imari Port before being exported and [3][h　　　　　　　　　　]. Imari ware has been developed since 1643 when Sakaida Kakiemon [4](e　　　　　) *aka-e*, a style of red painting. Such masterpieces, made in the 17th century and now called old Imari, have been prized both [5](d　　　　　) and [6](i　　　　　). European nobles bought works in the *kinrande* style — red painting with overlaying gold color accents — and used them for [7](d　　　　　) in their palaces. Imari ware in Kakiemon style also [8](a　　　　　) European pottery, and it was [9](a　　　　　) in various countries such as Meissen in Germany and Delft in the Netherlands.

Writing Task 2

Essay は「序論（Introduction）」「本論（Body）」「結論（Conclusion）」という三部構成になっており、それぞれに共通する特徴や、異なる役割があります。

◎ 共通	一貫性を保つために、文末の語句と次の文の冒頭が関連するように配置して、文と文を繋げます。同じ語句の繰り返しで読者に稚拙な印象を与えないよう、類語や上位語で言い換えます。節よりも句を用いることで、回りくどい文章を避け、一文を短く表現します。
◎ 序論	読者が最初に目にする部分です。興味関心を惹き付け、なるべく多くの読者に本論を読んでもらえるようにする役割があります。また、何を主題としているのかを明確に読者へ伝える役割も担っています。詳しくは Unit 12 を参照。
◎ 本論	主題に関する著者の考えとその根拠を示し、読者を納得させます。著者の主観が入ると説得力を損ねてしまうので、客観的に書かねばなりません。一人称・二人称代名詞や法助動詞を使わない、曖昧で主観的な形容詞を使う場合には必ず詳しい説明を添えるなどといった工夫が求められます。首尾一貫した内容にするため、次のような構造をもっています。 第一文で Topic と Controlling Idea を明示します（これを Topic Sentence といいます）。 第二文で論拠を抽象的にまとめます（これを Supporting Sentence といいます）。 第三文以降で論拠の詳細（Supports）を述べていきます。 論拠が複数ある場合は、再び Supporting Sentence を出し、Supports を添えます。 文と文のつながりを確保する際、本論に限っては、Topic として提示した語句（およびその類語）を再度文頭で用いることにより、一貫性を保ちながら書くことが可能となります。
◎ 結論	序論と本論で述べた内容をまとめ、著者の見解を示します。詳しくは Unit 11 を参照。

次の文章は、本論を意識して [Writing Task 1] の文章を作った際の初稿です。この時点ではどのような不備があり、それらが [Writing Task 1] の文章でどのように改善されているか、指摘してみましょう。

Imari ware is a kind of Arita ware. Imari ware is produced in the Arita area of Saga Prefecture and is named after Imari Port. Imari ware was developed in 1643 when Sakaida Kakiemon consolidated a style of red painting. Imari ware was also sold overseas. In particular, old Imari, made in the 17th century, is prized both at home and abroad. Old Imari in the "*kinrande* style" — red painting with overlaying gold color accents — was bought by European nobility and used for ornamentation in the palace. Kakiemon porcelain also influenced European pottery, and the style was introduced in various countries such as the German Meissen kiln and the Dutch Delft kiln.

Writing Task 3

日本のお土産としておすすめのものを紹介し、その魅力を伝える段落を作ってみましょう。

Traditional Crafts in Japan

A *Kokeshi* are charming. The traditional Japanese wooden doll with a spherical head and a cylindrical body emerged in hot spring areas across Japan as souvenirs around 1800. At that time, woodcrafters who usually made tableware and furniture started to carve the dolls as toys for girls. *Kokeshi* colors and shapes vary from region to region, which led to the product also becoming popular as a collectible. In addition to traditional style *kokeshi*, [   ] the creation of new types. These are not bound by tradition and incorporate unorthodox appearances; some are even modeled after ninja, samurai, animals, monsters, or animated characters. The charms of these dolls have contributed to an increase in *kokeshi* fans both domestically and internationally.

B *Kokeshi* possess a simple lovable beauty and *jizai okimono* have a meticulous realism. The two are supported by the craftsmanship of artisans who maintain the traditional arts. Each will continue to win admirers from all over the world.

C *Jizai okimono* are beautiful. These metal crafts which imitate the shapes of creatures like reptiles, birds, fish, or insects are so exquisitely designed that their joints or wings are able to move as naturally as if the object were alive. One example of this is the oldest existing *jizai okimono*, a model dragon composed of lifelike parts such as face, body, limbs, and talons, which was made in 1713. During the period of its creation, Japan's extended time without war compelled most armorers to change professions, leading some of them to use their metalworking skills to create *jizai okimono*. These artworks were exported to Europe and North America in the late 1800s and the Museum of Fine Arts in Boston currently has a *jizai okimono* dragon measuring 2.2 meters in length in its collection. Nevertheless, these metal artifacts remained relatively obscure in Japan, only gradually gaining in recognition following a domestic exhibition in the late 1900s.

D Many miniature representations of humans, animals, machines, buildings, and animated characters exist in the world in such forms as dolls, plastic models, or action figures. One such artifact, the Peter Rabbit doll, has been loved globally since the design registration in 1903 at the Patent Office in London. Japan has many traditional objects with lasting fame, two of which are *kokeshi* dolls and *jizai okimono*. The former have attracted widespread popularity for more than 200 years and the latter are works of art with a history stretching back more than 300 years. Why have these two been popular for such a long time?

---

spherical: 球状の　cylindrical: 円柱状の　collectible: 趣味の収集品　incorporate: 取り入れる
unorthodox: これまでにない　lovable: かわいらしい　meticulous: 細部まで行き届いた
craftsmanship: 職人の技　exquisitely: 極めて精巧に　lifelike: 生きているかのような　limb: 手足
talon: 爪　representation: 表現されたもの　the Patent Office: 特許局

1. A～Dの段落を正しい順に並べ替えましょう。

(　　) → (　　) → (　　) → (　　)

2. *"jizai okimono"* の言い換えとして用いられている名詞や名詞句を段落Cからすべて抜き出しましょう。

3. 下線部には、前の文と後の文にうまくつながるような工夫が施されています。"traditional style *kokeshi*" が前の文までの流れを受け、"new types" が次の文頭の "These" とつながります。このような文にするために、空欄には無生物主語とそれに対応する動詞が用いられます。では、次の直訳を参考に、この空欄を埋めてみましょう。なお、与えられた文字で始まります。そして、出来上がった英文を意訳してみましょう。

In addition to traditional style *kokeshi*, [r　　　　　　　　　　　　　　] the creation of new types.

［直訳：伝統的なこけしに加えて、近年は新型のその創造を目撃してきている。］

⇒［意訳：　　　　　　　　　　　　　　　　　　　　　　　　　　　　　　　］

4. 本文中で述べられているものは次のうちどれでしょうか。

a. Peter Rabbit was born in 1903.
b. All the traditional style *kokeshi* dolls have the same design.
c. Some new type *kokeshi* dolls are meant to create an impression of samurai.
d. There are more *kokeshi* enthusiasts in foreign countries than in Japan.

5. 本文中で述べられていないものは次のうちどれでしょうか。

a. *Jizai okimono* are made of metal.
b. The Museum of Fine Arts in Boston has a model dragon made in 1713.
c. *Jizai okimono* have been popular in Japan since the late 20th century.
d. In the Edo period, a lot of armorers were unable to avoid changing their careers.

Unit 11

Home Video Game Consoles from Japan

結論を書いてみる

1

2

3

4

5

6

Vocabulary 上の写真を参考に、「ゲーム」に関連しそうな語句を集め、表にまとめてみましょう。

名詞／名詞相当表現	形容詞／形容詞相当表現	動詞／動詞相当表現	副詞／副詞相当表現
・controller	・exciting	・play	・excitingly
・VR	・joyful	・use	・happily
・	・	・	・
・	・	・	・
・	・	・	・
・	・	・	・
・	・	・	・
・	・	・	・
・	・	・	・
・	・	・	・

Pre-Writing

〔　　〕内のヒントを参考に、空欄を補うのに最も適切な語句を書きましょう。（　　）には1語、［　　］には複数の語が入り、それぞれ与えられた文字で始まります。

1) Some video games are played (a　　　　　) or in (c　　　　　) with other players.
〔写真1より：他のプレイヤーと対戦したり協力したりできるゲームもある。〕

2) A boy is (p　　　　　) out a game at a (c　　　　　) sale.
〔写真5より：少年がワゴンセールのゲームソフトを選んでいる。〕

3) There are various types of (g　　　　　) (d　　　　　) and styles to play video games.
〔写真1～6より：ゲームをするには多くの種類の機器や方法がある。〕

4) To launch means to (i　　　　　) a product to the (m　　　　　) for the first time.
〔発売するとは、ある製品を世に初めて送り出すことを意味する。〕

5) Cumulative worldwide shipments show the [t　　　　　　　　　　] of a [p　　　　　　　　　　] sent from the factory to stores all over the world.
〔世界累計出荷台数とは、ある特定の商品がその工場から世界各国の販売店へと送られた総数である。〕

Drop-by

映画「アナと雪の女王」(2013) の原題は “Frozen” で、邦題と大きく異なっています。原題のままでは外国人には馴染みがなくイメージしづらかったり、別の意味にとらえられてしまったり、他国で既に商標登録されていたり、様々な理由で和名と英名を変える必要が出てくることもあるのです。これはゲームの世界でも起こります。例えば、サバイバルホラーゲームの金字塔「バイオハザード」は “Resident Evil”、コミュニケーションゲーム「どうぶつの森」は “Animal Crossing”、コピーライターの糸井重里氏が手掛けたことで知られる RPG「MOTHER 2」は “EarthBound”、アニメでも人気を誇る「ポケットモンスター」は “Pokémon”、そしてアクションゲームの王道「ロックマン」は “Mega Man” といった具合です。

Grammar

次に示す文章では、「the Nintendo Switch」という言葉が連続しています。文意を変えずにこの重複を解決してみましょう。下線部 1 は 2 語以上の名詞句に、下線部 2 は単文にしてみましょう。

In 2017, the "Nintendo Switch" was launched. [1)]The Nintendo Switch inherited the intuitive controls from Nintendo's past hardware and is able to be played both as a stationary game console and as a portable gaming device. [2)]The Nintendo Switch has been popular all over the world, so the Nintendo Switch has recorded sales of more than 60 million units in the four years since its release.

1) ....

2) ....

....

Writing Task 1

次の日本文に合うように、空欄を補うのに最も適切な語句を書きましょう。(　　) には 1 語、[　　] には複数の語が入り、それぞれ与えられた文字で始まります。

任天堂と SONY は携帯型ゲーム機にも強い。前者は「ゲームボーイ」を 1989 年に発売した。その 7 年後、「ポケットモンスター」が初めて発売され、今でもマリオに匹敵するほどの代表的な作品となっている。こうしたソフトが世界的に人気を博したためにゲームボーイは数回のデザイン変更が行われ、世界でのシリーズ累計販売数は 1 億台を突破。これは携帯型ゲーム機では初めてのことであった。一方、後者は 2004 年に「PlayStation Portable」を、2011 年にはその後継機である「PlayStation Vita」を発売した。それらの累計出荷台数も 1 億以上であった。任天堂と SONY の製品はこれからも世界中の人々を刺激してくれるはずだ。

Nintendo and Sony are both good at portable video game devices. The former launched the "Game Boy" in 1989. Seven years later, "Pokémon" was first [1](r　　　　　) and has become as [2](r　　　　　) a [3](c　　　　　) as Mario. Such software's worldwide popularity [4][s　　　　　　　　　　　　　　　　　　] of multiple generations of hardware. The global [5](u　　　　　) [6](s　　　　　) of the Game Boy were more than 100 million, which made it the first portable game [7](c　　　　　) to reach that number. The latter company put the "PlayStation Portable" on sale in 2004 and its [8](s　　　　　) model, the "PlayStation Vita," in 2011. The total sales of these devices also exceeded 100 million units across the globe. The products of Nintendo and Sony will [9](c　　　　　) people all over the world for years to come.

Writing Task 2 Essay の最終段落は「結論（Conclusion）」と呼ばれ、概ね次の 3 点が述べられます。

A. 主題文の言い換え または問題提起への解答	序論で主題を述べた場合は、それを別の表現に書き換えます。序論で問題提起をした場合は、その解答を書きます。
B. 本論の要約	本論各段落の Topic Sentence を、内容が変わらないようにしながらも、異なる語句を用いて書き換えます。
C. 著者の意見	本論から導き出される著者独自の見解を示します。読者への問い掛けという形式をとることもあります。

これら以外のことに触れてはいけません。例えば、序論や本論で触れられていない新しい情報が結論で出てきてしまうと、またそれについて説明しなければならず、結論が不必要に長くなってしまいます。Essay を通じて読者に伝えたいことは簡潔にまとめあげるように心がけましょう。著者の意見においては、法助動詞を活用すると “I think...” のような文言を使わずに表現することができます。また、上記の 3 点を書く順番は特に決まっておらず、扱う内容によっては 3 点すべてを盛り込む必要はありません。本論のまとめをより効果的に読者へ伝えるためにはどの順で何を述べるべきか、よく考えて書き、推敲を重ねましょう。

例えば、Unit 10 で登場した Essay の結論は以下のようになっています。1 ～ 3 は上記 A ～ C のそれぞれどれに該当するでしょうか。指摘してみましょう。

1) *Kokeshi* possess a simple lovable beauty and *jizai okimono* have a meticulous realism.
2) The two are supported by the craftsmanship of artisans who maintain the traditional arts.
3) Each will continue to attract admirers from all over the world.

また、 3 を次のように書き換えるとどのような印象を受けますか。

4) I think that each will continue to attract admirers from all over the world.
5) Each would continue to attract admirers from all over the world.

このような文章ではなく、3 のようになっているのには、理由があります。それは何でしょうか。

Writing Task 3 Unit 10 の Essay に関して、あなた独自の見解を結論として書いてみましょう。

Home Video Game Consoles from Japan

How someone spends their leisure time depends on the individual, whether it is reading books, watching movies, exercising, or shopping. Another way to engage in a pastime is playing games. Board games have been played over a period of thousands of years, and card games have been appreciated for centuries. Compared to them, home-based video games have a short history but are now familiar to people throughout the world.

Nintendo is a (1) video game company. It released its “Family Computer” (often referred to as a “Famicom” in Japan and as the “Nintendo Entertainment System” abroad) home video game console in 1983. At that time, it was innovative to be able to change cartridges to play different games on a single machine. One of them was “Super Mario Bros.” Launched in 1985, more than 40 million units of this software have been sold and about 62 million consoles were successfully marketed worldwide. Nintendo’s devices continued to evolve, with the “Wii” being released in 2006. Its approximately 15-centimeter, rod-shaped controller — the “Wii Remote” — had built-in sensors that allowed it to be used like a tennis racket or a sword. This unique controller attracted people who had never played video games, making the Wii an explosive best seller with more than 100 million units shipped. In 2017, the “Nintendo Switch” was launched. This machine inherited the intuitive controls from Nintendo’s past hardware and is able to be played both as a stationary game console and as a portable gaming device. Popular all over the world, the Nintendo Switch has recorded sales of more than 60 million units in the four years since its release.

Nintendo’s rivals have also made (2) progress. In 1994, Sony released the now iconic “PlayStation.” The company brought out popular game series such as “Resident Evil,” “Final Fantasy,” and “Dragon Quest” one after the other, contributing to the cumulative worldwide shipping of 100 million consoles. The “PlayStation 2” was launched in 2000 and sold for more than a decade worldwide. Its record 155 million global unit shipments make it the world’s best-selling console. Its successor, the “PlayStation 3” released in 2006, however, failed to surpass the Wii in sales. Sony followed by putting the “PlayStation 4” on the market in 2013, a console that sold more than 80 million units around the world in the following five years.

The newest technology of each period is reflected in its video games and they are constantly evolving. Japan’s gaming industry, led by Nintendo and Sony, will continue to provide pleasurable experiences to the world.

---

home video game console: 家庭用ゲーム機　home-based: 家庭用の　built-in: 内蔵の　inherit: 継承する
intuitive: 直観的な　stationary: 据置型の　iconic: 象徴的な　cumulative: 累計の　pleasurable: 楽しい

1. “home-based video games” の言い換えとして用いられている名詞や名詞句を本文中からすべて抜き出しましょう。

2. 空欄 1 および 2 に入る形容詞の組み合わせとして最も適切なものは次のうちどれでしょうか。

a. 1---unique 2---gradual
b. 1---popular 2---poor
c. 1---world-leading 2---excellent
d. 1---newborn 2---great

3. 本文第 2 段落で述べられている内容と一致するものは次のうちどれでしょうか。

a. Super Mario Bros. sold over 62 million units.
b. The Family Computer was the most famous stationary game console in the world.
c. The Wii is a portable gaming device.
d. The Wii Remote is a unique input device.

4. 本文第 3 段落で述べられている内容と一致するものは次のうちどれでしょうか。

a. The PlayStation is the best-selling game console in the world.
b. Both Final Fantasy and Dragon Quest hit the 100 million sales mark.
c. The cumulative worldwide shipments of the PlayStation 3 fell below 100 million units.
d. The PlayStation 4 sold as much as the PlayStation 2.

5. 本文の内容と合致するように、次の表の空欄を補いましょう。

機種名	Famicom	Wii	PlayStation	PlayStation 2
発売された年	(　　　　)年	(　　　　)年	(　　　　)年	(　　　　)年
累計出荷台数	約(　　　　)台	約(　　　　)台	約(　　　　)台	約(　　　　)台

Unit 12

Onsen Hot Springs

序論を書いてみる

1

2

3

4

5

6

Vocabulary 上の写真を参考に、「温泉」に関連しそうな語句を集め、表にまとめてみましょう。

名詞／名詞相当表現	形容詞／形容詞相当表現	動詞／動詞相当表現	副詞／副詞相当表現
· hot spring	· warm	· bathe	· comfortably
· spa	· hot	· take a bath	· slowly
·	·	·	·
·	·	·	·
·	·	·	·
·	·	·	·
·	·	·	·
·	·	·	·
·	·	·	·
·	·	·	·

Pre-Writing

〔　　〕内のヒントを参考に、空欄を補うのに最も適切な語句を書きましょう。（　　）には１語、［　　］には複数の語が入り、それぞれ与えられた文字で始まります。

1) A lot of monkeys are (r　　　　) (c　　　　) in an *onsen* hot spring.
〔写真２より「サル」を主語に：サルが気持ちよさそうに温泉につかっている。〕

2) An *onsen* hot spring seems to make some monkeys (f　　　　) (g　　　　).
〔写真２より「温泉」を主語に：サルが気持ち良さそうに温泉につかっている。〕

3) The spring (q　　　　) of Kusatsu Onsen in Gunma Prefecture is highly (a　　　　).
〔写真３より：群馬県の草津温泉の泉質は強酸性である。〕

4) A magma chamber is an (u　　　　) space where a lot of magma has (c　　　　).
〔マグマ溜まりとは、地中で多くのマグマが集まる部分のことである。〕

5) Efficacy means an ability to [w　　　　　　　　].
〔効能とは、好ましくない状況に対してうまく機能できる能力のことを指す。〕

Drop-by

上記３にあるように、群馬県の草津温泉は強酸性で有名です。殺菌力が強いので、戦国時代には、傷口を癒すために多くの兵士がここを訪れたという記録が残されています。そうした利点がある一方、大きな欠点もあります。強酸性の湯がそのまま川へ流入すると、その川の中では多くの生物が死滅してしまうのです。実際、草津温泉下流の湯川は「死の川」とも呼ばれ、生物が棲息できないだけでなく、農業用水として利用することもできませんでした。そこで 1964 年に酸性の川を中和する事業が始まりました。群馬県内で採取された石灰石を細かく砕き、その粉末を休むことなく中和のために川へ投入し続けます。その量は一日約 55t（年間約 20 万 t）にも上ります。こうして処理された水が一時的に品木《しなき》ダムに貯められ、そこで充分に中和された頃に下流の吾妻川《あがつまがわ》へと放水されるのです。こうして、魚が棲め、農業や工業にも利用できる河川へと生まれ変わった吾妻川は、やがて利根川と合流し、太平洋へと流れ込みます。日本三名泉のひとつに数えられる名湯には、このような背景もあるのです。

Grammar

次に示す３つの文章は、文法的には合っていますが前後の文とのつながりが悪く、読みにくくなってしまっています。文意を変えずに、つながりが良くなるように訂正してみましょう。

There are various kinds of *onsen* in Japan.
（日本にはさまざまな種類の温泉がある。）

It is good for health to bathe in *onsen* leisurely.
（温泉にゆったりと入浴することは健康に良い。）

So *onsen* is sometimes used for better health.
（そのため、健康増進のために温泉が利用されることもある。）

Writing Task 1

次の日本文に合うように、空欄を補うのに最も適切な語句を書きましょう。（　　）には１語、［　　］には複数の語が入り、それぞれ与えられた文字で始まります。

地球上には様々な形態で水が存在しています。例えば、北極や南極には多くの氷山があり、空に浮かぶ雲は雨や雪をもたらし、また、空気そのものも水分を含んでいます。それらは我々に様々な恩恵を授けてくれます。飲んだり、作物を育てたり、何かを洗ったりするなど、いろいろな方法で利用されます。そのうちの一つが入浴です。温泉とは、自然にあるいは人工的手段によって湯が湧き出ているところで、しばしば入浴施設として活用されています。温泉は驚嘆に値する場所なのです。

On Earth, water exists in several forms. For example, the 1.(p　　　　　　) 2.(r　　　　　　) have many icebergs, clouds in the sky carry rain and snow, and air itself also contains some moisture; all of which provide various benefits. Such as to drink, to 3.(g　　　　　　) 4.(c　　　　　　), or to wash something, water is used in numerous ways. One of them is to 5.(t　　　　　　) a 6.(b　　　　　　). Especially, hot springs — *onsen* in Japanese — are places 7.[w　　　　　　　　　　　　　　　　　　　　] and are often utilized as 8.(s　　　　　　) 9.(f　　　　　　) in Japan. They are quite wonderful places.

Writing Task 2 Essay の第一段落は「序論（Introduction）」と呼ばれ、下図のように書き方が決まっています。

『一般的情報／背景的知識』から入り
↓
徐々に読者の興味・関心を惹きつけ
↓
最後に『主題文／問題提起』

いきなり主題を提示すると、それに興味のない読者は続きを読んでくれません。したがって、誰にでも関係があるような広い話題（一般的情報や背景的知識）を紹介し、関心を持たせてから本題へと入ります。こうすることで本論の内容も伝わりやすくすることができます。

では、外国人学生に向けて「日本の温泉の良さ」を訴える Essay を書く場合、どのような序論がふさわしいでしょうか。次に示す (a) ~ (c) の書き出しから 1 つ選び、そこから【主題文】に繋がるように、【徐々に読者の興味･関心を惹きつける部分】に適した英文を 3 つ程度作成してみましょう。

【書き出し：誰もが知っているような一般的情報／背景的知識】

(a) On Earth, water exists in various forms.
(b) Human beings are not able to live without water.
(c) Humankind often seek pleasure.

【徐々に読者の興味・関心を惹きつける部分】

【主題文】

Writing Task 3 Writing Task 2 で作った序論に続く本論となるように、おすすめの温泉地を一つ取り上げ、それについて説明する段落を作ってみましょう。

Onsen Hot Springs

On Earth, there are many mountains. Prominent ones include Mt. Everest, well-known internationally for its height, and (A). Mt. Fuji is popular in Japan, a very volcanically active country. Volcanoes are important contributors to the existence of *onsen* hot spring areas, of which Japan has over three thousand. They are quite wonderful places.

Onsen are good for health. This fact is connected to the process that forms hot springs. Water from rain and snow that has seeped underground over many years is heated near magma chambers or by geothermal energy. This groundwater absorbs minerals such as sodium, magnesium, sulfur, calcium, and iron before it wells up naturally or is artificially extracted from the earth. These elements have a broad range of health-related effects. For example, chloride hot springs ease depression and sulfurous ones are efficacious in the treatment of some skin diseases. In order to experience such benefits, it is necessary to bathe regularly in *onsen* for one week or more. Called *toji*, which means *onsen* therapy in Japanese, this way of using hot springs was popular from the 17th to 19th centuries. For instance, Geto Onsen in Iwate hosted approximately two thousand people from all social strata during a single summer in the mid-18th century. Modern advances in medical technology and lifestyle changes, however, have shifted the main purpose of *onsen* to relaxation.

The process of bathing in an *onsen* is straightforward. First, before getting in the bath, use the provided bucket to pour heated water slowly over the feet, legs, abdomen, chest, back, arms, and head in turn. This procedure, called "*kakeyu*," reduces mental and physical strain caused by sudden temperature changes. Second, wash off the day's dirt and grime from the entire body. Doing this before getting in the bath keeps the *onsen* water clean. Once having washed, soak in the bathtub. While bathing, leave all towels out of the tub, which prevents any remaining soap or hairs on the fabric from spreading throughout the bath. Finally, do *kakeyu* again, and then wipe the entire body with a towel before entering the dressing room. This removes excess water and keeps the place from getting soaked.

Japan has various kinds of *onsen*, which differ from region to region. This sophisticated *onsen* culture means that most hot springs have a clean, pleasant environment. (B).

---

geothermal energy: 地熱　sodium: ナトリウム　sulfur: 硫黄　chloride: 塩化物　sulfurous: 硫黄の
efficacious: 効能がある　therapy: 治療　stratum (複 strata): 階層　straightforward: わかりやすい
abdomen: 腹部　strain: 負担　dirt: 汚れ　grime: 垢　dressing room: 脱衣所

1. “*onsen*” の言い換えとして用いられている名詞や名詞句を本文中からすべて抜き出しましょう。

2. 下線部の終わりがthe earthとなっていて、直後のThese elementsとうまくつながっていません。下線部の文意を変えないように、前後の文とうまくつながるように書き換えてみましょう。

   Water from rain and snow that has seeped underground over many years is heated near magma chambers or by geothermal energy. ......

   ...... These elements have a broad range of health-related effects.

3. 本文中で述べられていないものは次のうちどれでしょうか。

   a. *Onsen* have good effects on some diseases.
   b. There was a popular hot spring in Iwate.
   c. Both before and after taking a bath, *onsen* users should do *kakeyu*.
   d. *Toji* is still an essential part of Japanese lifestyle.

4. 序論の一部として空欄Aを補うのには、例えば「Mt. Kilimanjaro, whose name is now famous as a coffee-producing region」のような文が適切といえます。では、ほかにはどのような文が考えられるでしょうか。上記の例にならって英語で答えましょう。

5. 結論の一部として空欄Bを補うのに適切なものは次のうちどれでしょうか。

   a. Especially, Geto Onsen is a good hot spring town
   b. Foreigners must do *kakeyu* and *toji* in Japan
   c. People with some skin diseases should take a hot spring bath
   d. Enjoy this *onsen* life when you visit Japan

Unit 13

Folktales: Sensitivity to Things and Nature

集めた資料からアウトラインを作る

1

2
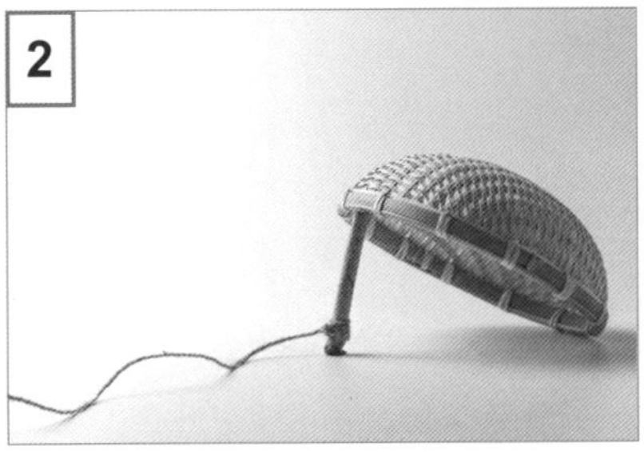

3

4

5

6

Vocabulary 上の絵や写真を説明するための語句を集め、表にまとめてみましょう。

名詞／名詞相当表現	形容詞／形容詞相当表現	動詞／動詞相当表現	副詞／副詞相当表現
· hut	· ancient	· capture	· stealthily
· snare	· snowy	· take a peep	· elegantly
·	·	·	·
·	·	·	·
·	·	·	·
·	·	·	·
·	·	·	·
·	·	·	·
·	·	·	·
·	·	·	·

Pre-Writing

〔　〕内のヒントを参考にして、空欄に適切な語句を書き入れましょう。(　)には与えられた文字で始まる１語が入ります。

1) There stands an (a　　　　　　) (c　　　　　　) in a snowy mountainous region.
〔写真１より：雪深い山間に一軒の古びた小屋がある。〕

2) A snare is a kind of (t　　　　　　) to catch (p　　　　　　) that is made of string or rope.
〔写真２より：輪縄とはひもや綱でできた獲物を捕らえるためのわなのことである。〕

3) An apparatus called a (l　　　　　　) is used for (w　　　　　　) yarn and making fabric.
〔写真３より：織機という装置を使って、糸を織り生地が作られる。〕

4) Someone is (p　　　　　　) inside through the mail (s　　　　　　) to see what is happening.
〔写真５より：誰かが郵便受けから覗き見をして、何が起きているのかを見ようとしている。〕

5) Two (c　　　　　　) are (s　　　　　　) through the air.
〔写真６より：二羽の鶴が空中を舞っている。〕

Drop-by

日本の昔話の中には、物語の展開があいまいなものが少なからず存在します。よく知られているように、浦島太郎は亀を助けたことにより、竜宮城に招かれ、厚遇を受けます。そこまでは、善行が報われるという教訓を読み取ることができるのですが、竜宮城から戻った浦島が知る人もいない孤独な状況で、玉手箱を開け、老人になってしまうという結末は、前半の流れからはおよそ想像がつかないものです。結果、浦島は一種の罰を受けるわけですから、これは報恩の話などではなく、人間の栄華はつかの間のものであることを戒める話なのでしょうか。本 Unit の Reading Section では、そのような日本の昔話のあいまいさについて学びます。ちなみに、各地に存在する浦島伝説が現在伝わる形に定まったのは室町時代とされ、この話は『古事記』の海幸彦と山幸彦の話を下敷きにしているという説があります。山幸彦は兄の海幸彦に借りた釣針を失くしてしまい、それを探して竜宮を訪れます。山幸彦は海神に気に入られ、海神の娘である豊玉姫と結婚します。陸に戻り、豊玉姫が子を産む段で、山幸彦は出産の場面を決して覗いてはならぬと釘を刺されます。しかし、彼は約束を破り、彼女が鰐（サメ）であることが発覚。正体が明かされたことを恥じた豊玉姫は寂しく海へと戻っていきます。

Writing Task 1

他の文献から文言を引用する場合に、書き換え(Paraphrase)を行うことがありますが、その練習として文学作品の英訳に挑戦してみましょう。次の日本語の文章に合うように、適切な語を(　　)に書き入れましょう。[　　]には、点線部の日本語の文を英語に直して入れてみましょう。

鶴の恩返し

昔、あるところにおじいさんとおばあさんが住んでいました。ある冬の日、おじいさんは鶴がわなにかかっているのを見つけ、かわいそうに思った彼は鶴を助けてあげました。同じ嵐の晩に、美しい若い女が一晩の宿を求めて、年老いた夫婦の小屋を訪ねてきました。そこに数日とどまる間、彼女は老夫婦の面倒をよく見、老夫婦の方も彼女を娘のようにかわいがりました。ある日、若い女は生地を織るための糸を手に入れてくるよう、おじいさんに頼みました。彼女はそれを手にすると、奥の部屋に閉じこもり、決して中を覗かないように言いました。それから、彼女は休みも取らず一心に布を織り続けました。老夫婦は彼女が美しい生地を織ってくれるおかげで、お金持ちになりました。しかし、彼女が働いている様子を見ようとして、ふと彼女との約束を破ってしまいました。部屋の中で布を織っていたのは義理の娘ではなく、羽の抜かれた鶴でした。彼女は自分の羽で生地を織っていたのでした。彼女は人間の姿に戻り、自分が以前、老人に助けられた鶴であることを明かし、鶴となって暗い夜空に飛び立っていきました。

The Grateful Crane

[1](O　　　　　) upon a time, in a certain place, there lived an old man and an old woman. On a snowy day, when the old man found a crane caught in a [2](s　　　　　), he felt sorry for the crane and set it free from the trap. The same stormy night, a beautiful young woman visited the [3](h　　　　　) of the old couple asking for [4](a　　　　　) for the night. She stayed there for a number of days, during which she took good care of them, and they kindly treated her as if she were their own daughter. One day, the young woman asked the old man to pick up yarn to weave cloth. After receiving it from him, she shut herself in the back room and ordered them not to [5](p　　　　　) inside. Then she [6](d　　　　　) herself to weaving with no rest. The aged couple became rich owing to the beautiful cloth that she made. [7][　　　　　　　　　　] Weaving cloth inside the room was not their [8](a　　　　　) daughter but a plucked crane! She wove cloth out of her own wings. Once again assuming human form, she [9](r　　　　　) that she was the crane who was spared by the old man and then, turning back into a crane, she flew away into the dark night.

Writing Task 2

「浦島太郎」のあらすじを英語で説明してみましょう。物語の説明なので、序論・本論・結論という流れにはせず、起承転結の流れを押さえます。いきなり詳しく書くのは難しいので、まずは物語の流れを4～5文程度で表現し、全体のアウトラインを整えましょう。小説や映画のあらすじは、物語に臨場感を付け加える意味で、現在形で説明するのが一般的ですが、昔話の場合は、過去形で説明しても構いません。

起：浦島太郎が竜宮 (the Kingdom Beneath the Sea) に案内されるまでの経緯を説明してみましょう。
承：亀に乗って竜宮を訪れる過程を説明してみましょう。
転：浦島が村に戻ることにする場面を説明してみましょう。
結：村に戻り、老人となる結末について説明してみましょう。

Writing Task 3

続いて、Writing Task 2 の内容に関して、起承転結それぞれを三文程度に膨らませて、より詳しいあらすじを作ってみましょう。下にあらすじの一部が与えられていますので、残りを埋めてください。

起：(introduction)　上で作成した文に物語の背景を説明する文を加えるとよいでしょう。

・
・One day, along the beach, he stumbled upon a sea turtle being bullied by naughty boys.
・

承：(development)　再び現れた亀とのやり取りや竜宮での体験を書くとよいでしょう。

・
・Accepting its attractive offer with great curiosity, he was put on its back and taken to a mysterious site.
・

転：(turn)　浦島が村に戻ることにする経緯や乙姫からの贈り物について書くとよいでしょう。

・For a long while, Taro lost track of time enjoying the paradisal life and beauty in *Ryugu*.
・
・

結：(conclusion)　変わり果てた村の様子や、玉手箱 (treasure box) を開けるに至る浦島の心境を書くとよいでしょう。

・
・He realized that an irrecoverably long time had passed during his short visit to *Ryugu*.
・

Folktales: Sensitivity to Things and Nature

Old tales reflect and are reflected in the morals and customs of the time and place of their origin. Therefore, a comparison of such long-inherited stories clarifies differences in national or regional cultural traits. According to psychologist Hayao Kawai, Western and Japanese tales exhibit a marked contrast. For example, the Cyprus folktale "The Three-eyed Man" and "The Village of the Nightingale" from Japanese folklore both have seemingly similar story lines, especially where (　　　　　　), but they are, in essence, opposite as two poles.

In "The Three-eyed Man," a woodman's daughter is banned from looking into the 101st chamber by her husband, who is in fact the titular three-eyed monster. She witnesses through the window of the forbidden room his excavating and devouring a dead body. Scared, she flees from him to be sheltered by the king in the castle. The king hopes to marry his son to her. Angry, her monster husband starts a pursuit to bring her back. Due to the prince's resourcefulness, the monster slips off some stairs and is eaten by beasts. The story ends with the [　A　] scene of the wedding between the woodman's daughter and the son of the king.

In "The Village of the Nightingale," a woodman failed to keep his promise to a beautiful woman. (1) (2) (3) (4) At this moment, the woman and the grand residence disappear. The story ends by depicting the man standing still, alone in the [　B　] forest.

In opposition to the Western story flowing forward toward a [　C　] climax, the ending of the Japanese folklore story is rather [　D　] and hence confusing. The story of "The Village of the Nightingale" does not advance at all; it ends with the man just standing where he stood at the start of the story. In short, it seems no development has occurred. This evanescent story, nevertheless, is not without substance. It can be interpreted as depicting a cultural sensitivity towards "nothing," or the occurrence of "something" in "nothing." This "nothing" exists as a part of the Japanese people's sense of beauty and capacity for feeling the pathos of things and nature.

"The Three-eyed Man":「三つ目男」（キプロス島の昔話）
"The Village of the Nightingale":「うぐいすの里」（日本の昔話）　opposite as two poles: 天と地の差がある
titular: 題名の　excavate: 掘り返す　devour: むさぼり食う　resourcefulness: 機知
evanescent: はかない　pathos: 悲哀

1. 第１段落の（　　）内には、「双方の物語の登場人物が相手との約束を破る」という内容が入ります。第２段落および第３段落の波線部にも注目しながら、英語で表現してみましょう。

....

....

2. 以下は文章中の（１）～（４）に入ります。下線を引いた語句にも注目して、この話のあらすじが分かるように正しく並び替えてみましょう。

(a) He enters the forbidden room out of curiosity and mistakenly drops three eggs, which break on the floor.
(b) It turns out that the woman is a nightingale and the eggs he dropped were her precious children that he killed.
(c) One day, the man accidentally stumbles upon a splendid mansion in the forest.
(d) The female host of the house warmly welcomes him but strictly orders him not to look into the seventh chamber.

(1) .... → (2) .... → (3) .... → (4) ....

3. 二つの物語の内容を踏まえて、文章中の［Ａ］～［Ｄ］に入る形容詞を考えてみましょう。

[A] ....　[B] ....

[C] ....　[D] ....

4. 第４段落下線部の著者の主張に沿うものは以下のうちのどれでしょうか。

(a) After all, nothing arises from nothing, so it does not mean anything to Japanese people.
(b) In Japan, something that actually exists has always been respected and valued more than something that does not.
(c) People in Japan have felt something from nothing and tried to express it in words or other representations.
(d) At all times, something abstract or nonfigurative has been most important to the Japanese.

Unit 14

Mythologies and Legends: Sense of Time

アウトラインに沿って下書きをしてみる

1

2

3

4
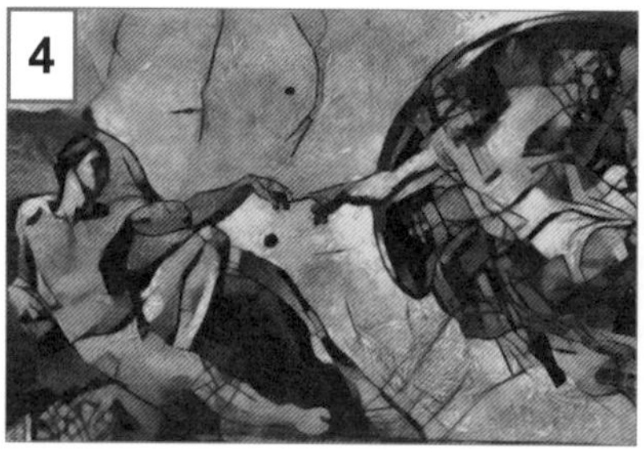

5

6

Vocabulary 上の絵や写真を説明するための語句を集め、表にまとめてみましょう。

名詞／名詞相当表現	形容詞／形容詞相当表現	動詞／動詞相当表現	副詞／副詞相当表現
・Takachiho Gorge	・holy	・deceive	・impressively
・Izumo Taisha Shrine	・miraculous	・expel	・magnificently
・	・	・	・
・	・	・	・
・	・	・	・
・	・	・	・
・	・	・	・
・	・	・	・
・	・	・	・
・	・	・	・

Pre-Writing

〔　〕内のヒントを参考にして、空欄に適切な語句を書き入れましょう。(　　)には与えられた文字で始まる1語が入ります。

1) Takachiho in Kyushu is considered a (c　　　　　) place to which the grandson of the Sun Goddess, (a　　　　　) (w　　　　　) other gods and goddesses, descended from heaven.
〔写真1より：九州地方の高千穂は天照大神の孫が他の神々を伴って降りてきた場所の一つとされる。〕

2) According to legend, the White Hare of Inaba (t　　　　　) sharks into forming a line for him to cross the sea but was severely wounded by them because of the (r　　　　　) of the lie.
〔写真2より：言い伝えによると、因幡の白兎は海を渡ろうとしてサメを騙し整列させたが、嘘がばれてしまったために大けがを負った。〕

3) One theory holds that Izumo Taisha Shrine was 96 meters high, (f　　　　　) (t　　　　　) (h　　　　　) (t　　　　　) it is now, and once the highest building in Japan.
〔写真3より：一説によると、出雲大社はかつて、今の4倍の96メートルの高さがあり、日本で最も高い建物であったと言われている。〕

4) Genesis depicts how Adam and Eve, by eating the (f　　　　　) fruit, gained knowledge of good and evil and (d　　　　　) a sense of shame.
〔写真5より：創世記には、アダムとイブが禁断の果実を食べたことにより、事の善悪を知り、羞恥心に目覚めた経緯が描かれる。〕

5) In Exodus, the sea is divided when Moses holds up a (s　　　　　), allowing him and the Israelites to (e　　　　　) from their Egyptian pursuers.
〔写真6より：出エジプト記において、モーセが杖を掲げると海が割れ、イスラエルの民はエジプト人の追手から逃れることができる。〕

Drop-by

日本の創世神話『古事記』においては、イザナギとイザナミの男女二神が、他の神々に命じられ、天から降り、アメノヌボコという矛で辺りに漂う混沌とした大地を掻き混ぜると、その矛から滴り落ちたものが積もって、オノゴロジマという最初の島が生まれます。この島は、自凝島と漢字表記されることがあり、「自ずと凝り固まった島」という意味があります。その後、イザナギとイザナミはこの島で結婚し、愛し合うことで、アハヂノホノサワケシマ（現在の淡路島）をはじめ、島々が生み出されます。最初にできたのが八つの島であったため、日本にはオオヤシマグニ（大八洲国）という古い呼称があります。一方、旧約聖書の創世記においては、第1日目に神はまず天と地を創造し、続いて光を作ることで昼と夜を分けます。その後、第7日目に休息を取るまでの間、次から次に、大地と海、植物と動物、太陽と月と星、そして自らの形に似せて人間を作り出します。最初の人間をアダムと呼びますが、アダム（Adam）という語はアダマー（Adamah）というヘブライ語の男性形であり、アダマーには「土」という意味があります。神が地面の土からアダムを作ったことから、このような名前が与えられたのではないかと考えられています。

Writing Task 1

次の日本語の文章に合うように、適切な語を（　　）に書き入れましょう。
［　　］には、点線部の日本語の文を英語に直して入れてみましょう。

『古事記』の冒頭で、イザナギはイザナミと共に順調に国作りを進めていくが、火の神カグツチを生んだことで、イザナミはひどい火傷を負い、死んでしまう。夫は愛する妻を追って黄泉の国を訪ねる。再会後、妻は夫に、共に元の世界に帰れるよう、黄泉の国の神に相談してみるが、待っている間、決して中を覗いてはならないと伝える。長く待たされたイザナギが中の様子を窺うと、イザナミの変わり果てた姿を目にする。イザナギはこれを恐れて逃げ出す。怒ったイザナミは夫を捕えようと大勢を遣わす。イザナギが黄泉の国と現世との境界にある坂まで来ると、そこに桃の木を見つける。彼が桃の実を取り、追手に投げつけると、みな退散していく。このエピソードが示すように、古来より桃には不思議な力が宿るとされ、人体の一部に似たその形状から生命や豊穣の象徴として捉えられることもある。地上の楽園を桃の漢字を使って桃源郷と言い、鬼を退治するのも他の果実ではなく「桃」太郎であるが、これらも桃が持つ肯定的なイメージと無関係ではないだろう。

In the beginning of an old Japanese myth, two deities, Izanagi and Izanami, worked together to form Japan. Unfortunately, however, Izanami got burned to death by giving [1](b　　　　　　) to Kagutsuchi, the god of fire. Izanagi visited the land of the dead to search for his wife's whereabouts. When they met again, the wife told her husband that she would consult with the god of the netherworld to let her go back to their home, adding that he must not look inside in the [2](m　　　　　　). Izanagi, bored of waiting, peeped furtively to see what was going on, and found his wife's badly decomposed dead body. Scared of this, Izanagi took flight. Mad at his betrayal, Izanami sent swarms of ghosts to [3](c　　　　　　) her husband. Izanagi managed to get to the entrance of the underworld and, just then, found a fruit-laden peach tree. As he [4](p　　　　　　) fruits and threw them at his [5](p　　　　　　), they scurried back in surprise. As this episode shows, it is traditionally believed that a mysterious power [6](d　　　　　　) within a peach. Because of its resemblance to a part of the human body, a peach is considered a symbol of life or [7](f　　　　　　). [8][　　　　　　　　　　] The hero of Japanese folklore who beat the band of [9](d　　　　　　), Momotaro, was born out of a peach, not other fruits. These examples illustrate some positive symbolic meanings of this delicious juicy fruit.

Writing Task 2

次ページでは、慣用句・ことわざを起点にして組み立てられた文章を読みます。そこで、日本や日本人の特徴を言い当てていると思われる表現を集めてみました。辞書を使って空欄に該当する英語表現を探し、日本語と英語の発想の違いを比較してみましょう。

明日は明日の風が吹く	Tomorrow is another day.
言わぬが花	(1)
過去は水に流す	Let bygones be bygones.
触らぬ神に祟りなし	(2)
知らぬが仏	(3)
出る杭は打たれる	(4)
長い物には巻かれろ	(5)
喉元過ぎれば熱さを忘れる	Danger past, God forgotten.

Writing Task 3

上に挙げた慣用句・ことわざを用いて、以下の Concluding Sentence を述べるために、(a) ～ (d) のような材料を用意しました。与えられた日本語の意味になるよう、[　　] 内に必要な英文を書き、これらを正しく並び替えましょう。そのうえで、この文章に不足している Topic Sentence を書いてみましょう。

Topic Sentence：

Through history, this island nation has taken completely different stances concerning diplomatic issues.

(a) For a certain short period before the dawn of the age of provincial wars, the Muromachi shogunate actively proceeded to trade with neighboring nations in order to keep track of international affairs.

(b) From the Nara to the middle Heian period, Japan was open to superior aspects of foreign countries' cultures, especially of the Tan Dynasty. [1][　　　　　　　　　　　　] (遣唐使が廃止されると、日本は実質上、外国との交流を断った。)

(c) [2][　　　　　　　　　　　　] (その後の明治時代にはいわゆる文明開化の音が鳴り響いた。)

(d) Throughout the Edo period, Japan was again closed off to the rest of the world, this time for more than two centuries. [3][　　　　　　　　　　　　] (欧米列強に開国を迫られ鎖国は終結を迎える。)

(　) → (　) → (　) → (　)

Concluding Sentence：

Japan has periodically undergone introverted and extroverted eras. These opposite attitudes were always caused by some kind of anxiety and necessity. Such serious concern, however, was sure to be forgotten and vanished in smoke over time, as the proverb "Danger past, God forgotten" goes.

Mythologies and Legends: Sense of Time

Do Japanese people easily lose interest in things? Once a sensational affair or accident occurs, TV programs actively cover it on the news, where it is enthusiastically received by viewers. After just one week or so, however, most Japanese people show less interest in the topic, which is completely forgotten after another week passes. Cultural critic Shuichi Kato expounds on such limited vision using the following expressions: [　　1　　] and [　　2　　]. These proverbs succinctly explain Japanese people's sense of time. Their attention is, he says, solely paid to the events of the present, not to the past nor the future.

One of the reasons for this trend is evident in the fact that Japan's oldest chronicles — the *Kojiki* and the *Nihon Shoki* — do not present a creation myth or eschatology. According to legend, the two deities Izanagi and Izanami stirred the primordial mass with a heavenly spear to form the Japanese islands. In other words, the existing universe was shaped by the god and goddess; the world was not created from [　　A　　]. In terms of the end, the old chronicles do not mention it at all. This perspective of a world without beginning or end is partly derived from the unchanging cycle of four distinctive seasons in this insular country.

People immersed in Western Christian cultures, in contrast, have a [　　B　　], not cyclical, sense of time with a definite beginning and end. Time necessarily goes in only one direction, from the past to the future. Exodus, for example, is the record of the persecuted Jewish people's harsh one-way journey from Egypt to the "Promised Land." Furthermore, the Bible explicitly accounts the creation and destruction of the world. The Old Testament book of Genesis starts with the line: "In the beginning God created the heaven and the earth." Concerning the end, Revelations, the last book of the New Testament, clearly describes the millennial kingdom following the return of Jesus Christ, the apocalypse after the final battle with Satan in Armageddon, the Last Judgement, and the subsequent perpetual world. In Christianity influenced cultures, present events are generally apprehended as existing within a certain span of time, which is closely related to and acutely aware of past and future events.

The above-mentioned myths and legends are eminently illustrative of different perceptions between both cultures about time and order. The point of this essay is not to say which is better. More important is whether each can appreciate its own specific cultural characteristics and, if necessary, learn something from the other. From a different point of view and with a wider perspective, it becomes possible to understand ourselves both more and better.

---

enthusiastically: 熱烈に　expound on ~: ～を詳説する　succinctly: 簡潔に　eschatology: 終末論
deity: 神　primordial: 原初の　immersed in ~: ～に浸された　persecuted: 迫害された
millennial: 至福千年の　apocalypse: 世の終末　Armageddon: ハルマゲドン（終末における善と悪の決戦）

第３段落における聖書の引用は King James Version による。

1. 空欄［１］と［２］には、「過去や未来よりも現在が大事である」という趣旨のことわざや慣用句が１つずつ入ります。第１段落の波線部につながるように、該当するものを英語で書き入れてみましょう。

［１］ .... ［２］ ....

2. 第２段落、第３段落の波線部をヒントに、［Ａ］と［Ｂ］に入る語句を考えてみましょう。

［Ａ］ .... ［Ｂ］ ....

3. 第４段落の下線部は “The point of this essay” という表現のせいで一人称に近い言い回しになっています。客観性を加えるために、他にどのような言い方が考えられるでしょうか。

....

....

4. 第２、第３段落の要点を整理して、本論のアウトラインを英語で作成してみましょう。

Paragraph 2

Topic Sentence:

Supporting Sentence 1:

Supporting Sentence 2:

Paragraph 3

Topic Sentence:

Supporting Sentence 1:

Supporting Sentence 2:

Unit 15

From a Part to the Whole: Sense of Space

下書きを推敲していく

1

2

3

4

5

6

Vocabulary 上の絵や写真を説明するための語句を集め、表にまとめてみましょう。

名詞／名詞相当表現	形容詞／形容詞相当表現	動詞／動詞相当表現	副詞／副詞相当表現
・ancestor	・narrow	・worship at a grave	・annually
・five-storied pagoda	・complicated	・rise up	・wholeheartedly
・	・	・	・
・	・	・	・
・	・	・	・
・	・	・	・
・	・	・	・
・	・	・	・
・	・	・	・
・	・	・	・

Pre-Writing

〔　　〕内のヒントを参考にして、空欄に適切な語句を書き入れましょう。(　　)には与えられた文字で始まる1語が入ります。

1) Mountainous regions in Japan seriously (s　　　　　) (f　　　　　) effects of depopulation.
〔写真1より：日本の山間の地域では、過疎化が深刻な問題になっている。〕

2) The height of the five-story pagoda of Shitennoji temple is (e　　　　　) (t　　　　　) that of a ten-to-twelve storied office building, and the view from the upper floors is spectacular.
〔写真3より：四天王寺の五重塔の高さは10階から12階建てのビルに相当し、上層階からは壮観な景色が楽しめる。〕

3) Donations are (p　　　　　) (i　　　　　) from all over the world for the reconstruction of burned-out Notre Dame Cathedral.
〔写真4より：焼け落ちたノートルダム寺院の再建のための寄付が世界中から続々と寄せられている。〕

4) The subway system in Tokyo is famous for its punctuality, but it is (f　　　　　) (f　　　　　) being accessible to first-time users because of its complexity.
〔写真5より：東京の地下鉄網は時間に正確なことで有名だが、複雑で、初めての人には決して利用しやすいものではない。〕

5) Urban areas in Japan, especially in the three biggest cities, (b　　　　　) (w　　　　　) various sizes of buildings.
〔写真6より：日本の都市、特に三大都市圏においては、大小のビルが林立している。〕

Drop-by

左右対称に美しさを感じますか？ヴェルサイユ宮殿は、「朕は国家なり」の有名なセリフを発し、絶対王政の礎を確たるものとした「太陽王」ルイ14世により1682年に建てられました。その建設に宮殿よりも多くの労力が注ぎ込まれたという噴水庭園には、自然の景色さえも一変させられる絶大な王の力が集約的に表現されています。庭園内に造られた「ラトナの噴水」の太陽神アポロンの像は王を、その足元に控える蛙や蜥蜴《とかげ》の像は貴族や農民を象徴するようです。ヴェルサイユ庭園はきれいな左右対称になっていますが、各々の部分より先に全体的な計画があればこそ、このような形が完成するのでしょう。同じ頃、日本は江戸時代。長期にわたる徳川政権がその足場を固めようとしていた時期です。幕府の拠点である江戸城の建設は、太田道灌により1457年に築かれた城を増改築する形で、1590年から1660年にかけて断続的に行われました。かくして出来上がった城内には左右対称な建物や部屋の配置は見当たりません。

Writing Task 1

次の日本語の文章に合うように、適切な語を(　　)に書き入れましょう。
[　　]には、点線部の日本語の文を英語に直して入れてみましょう。

日本文化と西洋文化の思考様式の違いは、例えば、日本語と英語の文や文章の構造を見ても明らかである。基本的に、日本語の文においては、まず主語が置かれ、次に修飾語、目的語が続き、最後に動詞が来る。したがって、文の趣旨は最後にようやく分かる。同様に、日本語の作文の導入部分は必ずしも文章全体のテーマを示すものではない。これに対して、英語の文では、動詞が主語の直後に来て、その後に目的語、修飾語と続く。つまり、これは補助的な要素が出て来る前に文の骨組みが提示されるということである。同様に、英語の作文においては各段落と文章全体の主題文が段落や文章の全体像をあらかじめ明確に示す。そのため、読者はそれらをしっかりと押さえることで、文章を正確に理解することができる。英語で作文を書こうとする者は以上のような基本的なルールに留意して、論理的・体系的に文章を組み立てることが重要である。

The different thought patterns of Japanese and Western cultures are [1](a　　　　　　), for example, in the differences in the structure of sentences between the Japanese and English languages. Essentially, in a Japanese sentence the subject comes first, the modifiers second, the object third, and the verb last. Thus, the [2](i　　　　　　) and purpose of the sentence cannot be fully understood until the end. Similarly, the introductory parts of a Japanese essay do not necessarily include the theme of the whole of the passages. In English sentences, in [3](c　　　　　　), the verb comes right after the subject, and is then [4](f　　　　　　) by the object and the modifiers. This means that the [5](f　　　　　　) of the sentence is presented before its [6](s　　　　　　) items. Likewise, the topic sentence and the thesis statement clearly indicate in advance the whole picture of a paragraph and paragraphs in English [7](c　　　　　　). Grasping these key sentences, therefore, gives readers [8](a　　　　　　) and firm understanding of the writing.
[9][　　　　　　　　　　　　　　　　　　　　　　　　　　　　　　　　]

Writing Task 2 各自が用意したテーマ（教員から指示があったテーマ）で、実際に 300 語程度の Essay を書いてみましょう。

Writing Task 3 Writing Task 2 で書いた Essay が、これまでに学習したポイントに合致しているか確認してみましょう。特に以下のポイントをチェックし、必要に応じて文章を書き直しましょう。

序論

- □ 想定される読み手に関連がありそうな広い話題から入り、読み手の関心を引きつけられていますか。
- □ 段落の末尾に、主題文または問題提起が書かれていますか。
- □ 本論の最短段落よりも短くまとまっていますか。

本論

- □ 第一文目に Topic と Controlling Idea をこの順序で含む Topic Sentence が示されていますか。
- □ Supporting Sentence は Controlling Idea の根拠となる事柄をまとめた内容になっていますか。
- □ それに続く文章（Supports）で Supporting Sentence の根拠となるデータや客観的事実が示されていますか。
- □ 文末の語句とそれに続く文の冒頭が、関連性をもってつながっていますか。
- □ 主観的な表現を避けて、論証が進められていますか。

結論

- □ 次の項目のいずれか少なくとも一つが盛り込まれていますか。
  1. 主題文の言い換え／問題提起に対する解答
  2. 本論の要約（各 Topic Sentence の言い換え）
  3. 著者独自の意見・見解・提言
- □ 序論・本論で言及されていない新しい情報が書かれていませんか。
- □ 本論の最短段落よりも短くまとまっていますか。

全体

- □ 同じ語句が不必要に連続して使用されていませんか。
- □ 句を使用せず、接続詞や関係詞などで必要以上に文が長くなっていませんか。
- □ don't や isn't のような縮約形を使用していませんか。
- □ 文頭で and や but などの等位接続詞を使っていませんか。
- □ 教員に指定された書式がある場合、それを守って書かれていますか。

From a Part to the Whole: Sense of Space

Japan is bounded by water on every side, and almost all small areas of flat ground are separated by mountains and rivers. Partly because of this insularity and geographical limitation, Japanese people have long and strongly been conscious of the boundaries of everything in their daily lives and therefore have fostered (i) a highly developed sense of belonging within boundaries. This narrow mental attitude of the Japanese people has often been regarded as exclusive or clannish. In this age of internationalization, however, such an isolated and somewhat outdated image of Japan is slowly but steadily changing for the better. Meanwhile, the unique Japanese spirit still appears and reappears in various forms in various situations.

According to Shuichi Kato, Japanese people, on the whole, tend to focus exclusively on the events in their immediate vicinity with an intense group consciousness. For example, during the *Obon* festival and the vernal and autumnal equinoctial days, visitors to graves offer prayers to things far away from this life at first glance. However, in fact, they just are welcoming ancestral souls that return from *higan* (that world) rather than making offerings to the spirits of ancestors from *shigan* (this world). This aptly illustrates the tendency of Japanese people to grasp things from [A]. Similarly, ancient Japanese shrines and temples are historically shorter than Western churches with their upward-thrusting spires. Even in relatively taller structures like the five-storied pagoda, architectural emphasis is put on horizontal lines instead of vertical lines, so the structure looks [B]. This design choice partially comes from the fact that Japanese people do not pray to a distant celestial world but live with multitudinous gods in their surroundings.

(ii) Japanese culture placing high importance on near events when considering the makeup of things naturally puts more emphasis on "a part" than "the whole." In general, the whole preexists (or supports) the parts in Western cultures, while the whole is composed of (or is supported by) the parts in Japanese culture. The Japanese tendency to think from a part to the whole is apparent in housing architecture and urban planning. In traditional dwellings or large public constructions in this country, additional rooms, structures, and stories were attached one after another to an original building. Likewise, modern urban planning such as the construction of skyscrapers, underground shopping arcades, and subway systems is carried out randomly without any overall long-term vision.

This shortsighted attitude of Japanese culture is not necessarily a bad thing. The limited geographical environment of this island nation has nurtured the originality and ingenuity of the people living in it. In turn, this leads to the complicated and intricate architectural and spatial expressions found in the country. From (1) to (2) and (3), illustrations of Japanese cultural uniqueness are sure to attract attention from people around the world.

---

insularity: 島国性、狭量さ　clannish: 排他的な　vicinity: 近辺　vernal equinoctial day: 春分の日
autumnal equinoctial day: 秋分の日　upward-thrusting: 上方に突き出た　celestial: 天上の
multitudinous gods: 多数の神々、八百万の神　ingenuity: 創意工夫

1. 下線部（ i ）は、何への帰属意識を指しているのでしょうか。各自で考え、英語で例を挙げましょう。

2. 第２段落の［ A ］と［ B ］に入る語句は何でしょうか。波線部を参考に考えてみましょう。

［ A ］ ［ B ］

3. 下線部（ ii ）の要点を押さえているのは以下のどれでしょうか。

(a) Japanese people do not have any interest in the whole of something.
(b) Japanese people's way of thinking is that parts accumulate to form the whole of something.
(c) People in Western cultures pay no attention to details of things.
(d) Japanese people and Western people have a lot in common in regard to the perception of things.

4. 第３段落までの内容を押さえたうえで、第４段落の（ 1 ）～（ 3 ）に入る語句を考えてみましょう。

(1)

(2)

(3)

Writing Skills for Readers: Vocabulary to Essay on Japan

日本文化の再発見から学ぶEssayの書き方・読み方 [B-929]

１刷 2021年１月31日
３刷 2022年８月26日

著 者 日本英語表現学会テキスト研究部会
新井 巧磨 Takuma Arai
梅宮 悠 Yu Umemiya
大橋 文香 Fumika Ohashi
佐竹 幸信 Yukinobu Satake
田村 亮 Ryo Tamura
ウェザリー ウイリアム William Weatherly

発行者 南雲一範 Kazunori Nagumo
発行所 株式会社 南雲堂
〒162-0801 東京都新宿区山吹町361
NAN'UN-DO Co., Ltd.
361 Yamabuki-cho, Shinjuku-ku, Tokyo 162-0801, Japan
振替口座：00160-0-46863
TEL: 03-3268-2311（営業部：学校関係）
03-3268-2384（営業部：書店関係）
03-3268-2387（編集部）
FAX: 03-3269-2486

編集者 加藤 敦／堀田 華
装 丁 銀月堂
組 版 Office haru
検 印 省 略
コード ISBN978-4-523-17929-0 C0082

Printed in Japan

E-mail nanundo@post.email.ne.jp
URL https://www.nanun-do.co.jp/